SUSTAINABLE BY DESIGN

ECONOMIC DEVELOPMENT

&

NATURAL RESOURCES USE

BY

J.C. WANDEMBERG BOSCHETTI Ph.D.

Doctor of Philosophy in Socio-Ecological Systems

This research is focused on the identification and enhanced understanding of system ic issues in general (e.g., econom ic, organizational, environm ental) and hum an behavior in particular (e.g., participation, com m itm ent, responsibility) leading to resource m isallocation, over-exploitation, and unsustainable project outcom es.

The approach used transcends conventional neoclassical welfare econom ics. Hum an behaviors, such as participation and com m itm ent, and factors that influence and m otivate those behaviors (e.g., econom ic, organizational, environm ental) are central to any understanding of how to design for sustainable outcom es and for the m itigation/elim ination of negative externalities.

Research has shown that all organizations (form al or inform al) m ake a conscious or unconscious choice between two organizational structures, (1) bureaucratic and, (2) participative-dem ocratic. The effects of this choice on individual behaviors (goal-seeking vs. ideal-seeking), and the environm ental m anagem ent im plications thereof, are profoundly different. A review of literature on projects conducted throughout the world correlates project effectiveness (i.e., success in m eeting project objectives and m aintaining the desired outcom es) and negative outcom es (i.e., failure to m eet project objectives and m aintain the desired outcom es, m isallocation of resources and negative externalities) with specific types of project organizational structures.

In this research, I analyzed nine developm ent projects undertaken in Ecuador. The organizational structure and perform ance of the Ecuadorian projects were rated by the respondents by m eans of a survey instrum ent divided into 3 sections. The m eans of the scores obtained in sections II and

III were used to construct a Project Performance Index (PPI) and an Organizational Structure Index (OSI), respectively, for each project. The PPI and OSI scores, for the nine Ecuadorian projects, were then used to conduct a simple linear regression. The results from this analysis indicate a strong linear positive correlation ($R2 = .73$; $F = 19.33$; Significant $F = .0032$) between project performance and organizational structure. The hypothesis that an organizational structure that more closely resembles a participative democracy encourages high project performance and outcome sustainability is strongly supported. The hypothesis that organizations that more closely resemble bureaucratic structures (regardless of their phenotypic design) translate into less than optimal performance and unsustainable outcomes is also strongly supported. Keywords: Design Principles, Economic Development, Externalities, Goal-seeking, Ideal-seeking, Participation, Sustainable System, Sustainability.

TABLE OF CONTENTS

NGO Non-governmental Organization

PDM Participatory Decision Making

PDW Participative Design Workshop

SC Search Conference

SO4 Strategic Objective #4

SUBIR Sustainable Uses for Biological Resources

TNC The Nature Conservancy

UNDC United Nations Development Commission

UNEP United Nations Environment Commission

USAID United State Agency for International Development

WCED World Commission on Environment and Development

WRI World Resources Institute

WTO World Trade Organization

1. INTRODUCTION

1.1 A World with Increasing Relevant Uncertainties and System Discontinuities

The world in which we now live is often referred to as dynamic and turbulent. This turbulent environment, characterized by a high degree of relevant uncertainty and system discontinuities, was first noticed as emergent in 1962 by Emery and Trist and described as Type IV in their seminal work "The Causal Texture of Our Environments" (1965). Within this type of environment, deterministic linear thinking and mechanistic problem-solving approaches are proving insufficient to deal with the increasing complexities of our times, particularly regarding social, economic and environmental issues (Funtowics and Ravetz, 1991). So, how do we deal with these issues within an increasingly dynamic, uncertain, interconnected, and complex environment? Although the limitations of this research are obvious, such as the relatively small sample of projects analyzed, the value of the alternative offered here cannot be diminished.

1.2 Environmental Sustainability

The importance of environmental sustainability (however defined), as the foundation for social, institutional, and economic well-being, is becoming globally recognized. The need for rethinking development approaches in a way that best guarantees environmental, social, institutional, and economic sustainability has been acknowledged and documented by researchers, social scientists, and development agencies throughout the world (Anderson, 1991; Beckerman, 1992; Brown et al., 1993; Daly, 1993; Homer-Dixon et al., 1993; Toman, 1994; Upreti, 1994; Utton et al., 1976; Young, 1992). Recognition is the easy part. What remains to be determined is the means by which social, economic, and environmental sustainability can be best achieved. Environmental degradation, such as deforestation, desertification, wetlands destruction, air and water pollution, keep reaching unprecedented proportions. This is particularly evident in some parts of the "less developed" world (Bos, 1994; Brown, 1993; Douthwaite, 1993; Duchin and Lange, 1994; Hudson, 1991). The increasing pressure of global free trade and the inefficient use and allocation of natural resources in these parts of the world impose ever-greater constraints on the livelihoods and well-being of local peoples. Negligible man-made capital assets combined with non-existent or ill-defined property rights, inaccessible financial services, inadequate or non-existent safety nets in time of disaster or stress, and inability (or unwillingness due to inability) to participate in decision-making, forces people to adopt ever shorter time horizons. These forced decisions favor immediate needs and goals over long-term objectives or ideals and most often contribute to a downward spiral of economic, social, institutional, and environmental degradation (IFAD, 1995). A focus on what may constitute the best means to deal with uncompensated effects (i.e, negative externalities) and unsustainable project outcomes associated with development programs must become a priority in local and global development strategies. This focus was somewhat acknowledged in 1987 by the World Commission on Environment and Development (WCED, 1987), or Bruntland Report, and again in June 1992 at the Rio Summit by the United Nations Development Commission (UNDC, 1992) when it was stated that "Democracy at all levels of government, the involvement of community groups and non-governmental organizations, and equal rights for all are key to sustainable development." However, it does not seem feasible to translate this statement into actions, and much less to accomplish a "sustainable development," without a conceptual knowledge of human organizations and their underlying behaviors.

1.3 Neoclassical Welfare Economics

Neoclassical welfare economics has been highly criticized for centering on the concept of general economic equilibrium (Cordato, 1992; Ormerod, 1994; Prychitko, 1993; Soros, 1997). This concept has been developed in such a way as to have little, if any, relevance in the real world of policy making (Cordato, 1992; Soros, 1997). The model of general equilibrium is an abstract answer to an abstract question, i.e., whether or not a decentralized economy, relying only on price signals for utility and profit maximization, can achieve general equilibrium (Prychitko, 1993). The premise of a market clearing equilibrium according to Ormerod (1994) should be considered an unacceptable principle for economic theory. Mathematical analyses have shown that uncertain, incomplete, and/or late information can give rise to non-linear behavior in markets considered otherwise ideal (Ibid). Ormerod also argues against the "rationality" of economic units (i.e., self-interest in micro-economics and rational expectations in macro-economics) for this rationality, in actuality, is neither definable nor evident and thus not very meaningful as a general postulate for economic theory (Ormerod, 1994). Economists have abstracted almost completely from real-world efficiency problems facing humans by constructing static, deterministic, and utopian models of efficiency (Cordato, 1992; Soros, 1997). Rather than making economic models reflect reality, economists have tried to force reality to reflect their models. The determinate mathematical solution of competitive equilibrium, that mathematical economics has shown to exist in the abstract world is, according to Ormerod (1994), mathematically unsound and conflicting with observed events. Even if this mathematical solution were flawless, one cannot translate this static equilibrium to an existing economy based upon theoretical and unrealistic assumptions. Some of these utopian assumptions follow:

- Perfect information that would allow for perfectly rational utility-maximizing and profit maximizing choices.

- Perfect competition, whereby rivalry over profits is exhausted.
- Full equilibrium that captures marginal costs and benefits.
- Nonexistent monopolistic forces which can individually manipulate prices.
- Atomistic individualism which implies economic agents free from traditions, customs, and non-pecuniary interests.

If these assumptions (and others, such as appropriate convexity conditions to allow for comparable marginal rates of substitution) are met, then it is said that the economy in question has reached general equilibrium and is efficient, or Pareto optimal, i.e., further changes in production and exchange conditions will not further increase the total welfare of society (Atkins and Lowe, 1977). But general equilibrium, if at all possible in a timeless, static and abstract world, is not possible to produce in the real world. The impossibility of achieving perfect knowledge is one example. Ormerod (1994) refers to substantial evidence (Partha Dasgupta and Geoffrey Heal's book entitled Economic Theory and Exhaustible Resources) supporting the impossibility of fully informative price systems. Perfect knowledge may be possible only in a closed, timeless, static and non-existent system, but it is impossible within non-equilibrium, open, and real systems (Pepper, 1942). For example, many of the results obtained from the standard model of competitive equilibrium do not hold when uncertainty is introduced into the theoretical framework (Ormerod, 1994). Ormerod also refers to David Newbery and Joseph Stiglitz's proof that the standard model of competitive equilibrium is not true (Ibid). This is not to say that "free-market" policies are useless, but that the real world is far more complex than allowed for in the conventional economic model of rational expectations and competitive equilibrium. In lieu of perfect knowledge, which is non-attainable, a high degree of communication between the actors within a system ought to be sought. This would allow for the existing knowledge to be maximally and optimally available to all.

1.4 Market Failure or Institutional/organizational Failure?

The inefficient use and allocation of natural resources (e.g., negative externalities) which decrease social welfare, threaten long-term sustainability and the short-term viability of development efforts, manifest themselves, inter alia, in such issues as deforestation, soil erosion, air and water pollution at the local level, and in ozone depletion, global warming, and desertification at the global level. Inefficient resource use and allocation of resources is most often referred to in terms of "market failure."

Economists argue that environmental degradation results from the failure of the market system to put value on the environment. This market failure appears as negative externalities reflected by natural resources overuse and eventual degradation (Cropper and Oates, 1992; Daly and Cobb, 1989). The solution offered is to put a price on environmental goods and services. This approach assumes that environmental, social, and economic failures can be solved through the superimposition of an abstract economic construct called a market. The "market," however, is an abstract device for rationalizing an aggregate of human behaviors in one sphere of human interactions. Markets are, most often, the predictable results of institutional/organizational factors which, directly and indirectly, impose and reinforce patterns of individualistic thinking and behavior. People create markets, or keep them from being created or functioning efficiently. People are at the core of environmental degradation/conservation. To accept as given, and to focus on the market and its failures, may only reinforce the very values that are at the root of most social, institutional, environmental, and economic problems, limiting, a priori, the search for answers (Beder, 1996).

It has been argued that markets, far from being free or operating efficiently (through the "invisible hand") to allocate resources in the interests of society, are dominated by few market forces (e.g., large firms and corporations), also referred to as the "invisible elbow" (Jacobs, 1991). This "invisible elbow" aims at maximizing private profit while not necessarily trying to reduce, much less eliminate, negative externalities (Templet, 1995; White, 1992). Some even argue that environmental economics, with its focus on "efficiency," is a deliberate ploy by those in power to counteract any possibility of social and political change arising from environmental concerns (Beder, 1996).

Market failures, responsible for the generation of factor market distortions, such as subsidies, taxes, and quotas, cause the divergence between private and social marginal costs. This divergence creates an incentive for profit-maximizing firms to transform private costs into external costs (i.e., negative externalities), shifting the market supply curve to an artificially low point based only on private costs. When social costs are ignored, a production subsidy of sorts is created which leads to artificially low product prices and excessive production and pollution. Inefficient allocation, production, and consumption of resources lead to social, economic, institutional, and environmental degradation (Daly, 1968; Perrings, 1987; Templet, 1994). The failures to eliminate or reduce the divergence between private and social costs and uncompensated effects (i.e., negative externalities) associated with development programs do not seem inherent to specific regions or communities. Nor do they appear to be due to financial constraints, poor science/technology, or environmental circumstances.

These divergences do seem to be consistently associated with organizational or institutional structures based on a "centralized mindset" (Resnick, 1997) and "mechanistic" or "organistic" world views (i.e., close-system perspectives) (Pepper, 1943). These close-system perspectives and a centralized mindset seem characteristic of most development

projects (Hudson, 1991; Nowak et al., 1995; Wood, 1976).
Consequently, negative externalities are not be the product of
some technical failure of an abstract economic construct called
a market, but a consequence of inadequate human behaviors
and interactions. Hence, the need for the establishment of an
organizational/institutional environment conducive to
adequate human behaviors and interactions. 1.5 Ecuador's
Environmental, Social, and Economic Degradation At the
heart of Ecuador's social, economic, and environmental
degradation lie "market failures" evidenced by two digit
inflation, crime, unemployment, air and water pollution,
deforestation, erosion, and sedimentation of hydroelectric
dams. These "market failures" are the legacy of economic
development models that lacked the capacity to internalize,
reduce, or eliminate negative externalities.

In Ecuador, as in most countries, economic and political
aspects have historically taken precedence over social and
environmental concerns. This is evidenced by the progressive
reduction of the health and education budgets relative to other
allocations (e.g., foreign debt servicing, defence) and the
paucity of resources allocated to combat environmental
degradation (Southgate and Whitaker, 1994). Despite
Ecuador's nation-wide deforestation (estimates range from 60
thousand hectares/year to more than 340 thousand
hectares/year), air and water pollution (e.g. Taura syndrome),
mangrove destruction, desertification, no solution seems to be
forthcoming (Ibid). Ecuadorian governments have been unable
to protect even the Galapagos Islands, patrimony of humanity,
from vested interests more concerned with commerce and
short-term gains (e.g., tourism, fishing) than with the long
term sustainability of the islands. Although it can be argued
that governments try to protect the integrity and well-being of
their citizenry, since the globalization of "free" markets,
governments have been under pressure by forces such as the
Multilateral Agreement on Investment (MAI), and the World
Trade Organization (WTO) to focus mainly on global
economic variables while paying less attention to social,

human and environmental factors at the local level. The focus
on economic variables (e.g., monetary and fiscal policies,
especially at the macro level) has proved to be relatively
successful in short-term gains (e.g., short-term inflation
reduction). However, short-term economic gains have not
been maintained and have done little to address Ecuador's
environmental degradation, let alone its social ills. The
importance of addressing Ecuador's long-term internal and
external economic factors within a global context cannot be
over emphasized. Issues such as discriminatory macro and
micro sectoral policies, factor market distortions, financial
sector repression, inadequate investment in the scientific base
of the rural economy, foreign debt servicing, and market
globalization are important to the nation's survival (Southgate
and Whitaker, 1994). How these internal and external factors
are addressed needs to be reconsidered if "survival" is to have
any meaning.

1.5.1 Economic Policies

Past and current economic policies have stimulated, and
continue to stimulate, profit maximizing firms to transform
private costs into social costs (i.e., negative externalities). This
private-cost shifting results in a type of production subsidy
that leads to artificially low prices (e.g., timber prices) which
stimulate over-consumption and more negative externalities,
i.e., more deforestation, erosion, sedimentation and
desertification. Such subsidies have a domino effect,
producing low extraction fees, quotas and bans for export, and
other factor market distortions. This would explain the strong
correlation between the rate of logging worldwide and forest
ownership patterns (Marchak, 1995). The smaller the number
of wood lot owners, the greater the logging rate (Ibid).
One of the many environmental problems facing Ecuador is
deforestation. However, according to some (e.g., Ecuadorian
Wood Industry Association), deforestation is not the main
problem facing the forestry sector in Ecuador, but are the
following:

· Absence of a forestry zoning plan · Obsolescence of the existing forestry law · Lack of up-to-date forestry inventories and accounting · Lack of credits or incentives for sustainable forestry · Inaccessibility of forest lands for permanent use · Undefined areas for permanent forestry use · Lack of a maintained reforestation plan at the national level · Absence of a forestry culture in the country · Use of inefficient technologies · Lack of technological R & D

It is important to notice that seven out of these ten points deal directly with organizational or institutional problems.

1.5.2 The SUBIR Project

To help stop and reverse environmental degradation in Ecuador, the United States Agency for International Development (USAID) undertook several strategic objectives (SO). One of these, namely, Strategic Objective #4 (SO4) aims at promoting the sustainable use of the natural resource base, the conservation of biological diversity, and the control of pollution (USAID, 1996). The primary vehicle used by USAID for supporting SO4 is the Sustainable Uses for Biological Resources or SUBIR project (Ibid). The SUBIR project was developed "to identify, test and develop economically, ecologically, and socially sustainable resource management policies and models in three Ecuadorian parks and their buffer zones in order to preserve biodiversity and improve the economic well-being of local communities through their participation in the management of renewable natural resources" (USAID, 1996:6). The primary constraint facing SO4, according to USAID (1996), is the magnitude of the problem of environmental degradation and the complexity of interests which involve indigenous groups, petroleum and timber companies, environmental NGOs and others. An additional constraint identified by USAID is the Government of Ecuador's weak ability to follow through on policy reforms and laws already approved (Ibid).

1.5.3 Institutional/Organizational Issues

Much of USAID's analysis of constraints confronting SO 4 (as of May, 1996) can be characterized as institutional or organizational--as opposed to technical--issues. USAID (1996) has acknowledged that, unless people change their behavior with respect to natural and man-made resource use, there is little hope for sustainable development. Everyone involved in development activities has, on more than one occasion, heard or said, "we could take care of the problem immediately if the people would only cooperate/participate." The people in general (community members, volunteer groups, project teams), and their behavior in particular, and how they relate to each other (i.e., organization) are crucial to the success or failure of a collective endeavor. This is particularly true given the dynamic and turbulent environment in which most humans are living. Yet, this virtually axiomatic statement has not translated into efforts to investigate the issue commensurate with its importance. The reasons for not doing so may relate to relative familiarity and ease of search for technical solutions, and to lack of conceptual clarity of alternative approaches such as examining the role of the extant organizational structures.

1.6 The Importance of Organizational Structure

Lippitt and White's (1943) seminal work on group climates demonstrated that all human organizations embody one of only two genotypic and fundamentally technical organizational structures: (1) Bureaucratic; and, (2) Participative Democratic. Emery (1993) refers to bureaucratic and participative democratic structures as the first and second design principles, respectively (Ibid). The bureaucratic, or First Design Principle (DP1), has a dominant hierarchy inhabited by specialized individuals with highly defined tasks. In this type of structure the redundancy, essential to the flexibility, adaptability, and viability of all systems is incorporated through the addition of redundant "parts" (i.e., individuals with the same skills) (Emery, 1993). This accounts for the technical name "redundancy of parts" (Emery, 1993). It has also been called "the Megamachine" (Mumford, 1967). The participative democratic, or Second Design Principle (DP2), has a non-dominant hierarchy or flat organizational structure inhabited by individuals who are highly specialized, but multi-skilled. In this type of structure, the redundancy, essential to the flexibility, adaptability, and viability of all systems, is incorporated through the process of multiskilling (i.e., individuals with different [but redundant] functions). This accounts for the technical name "redundancy of functions" (Emery, 1993).

Organizational researchers have found that bureaucratic (DP1) and participative democratic (DP2) structures have profound and predictable effects on the people who live and work within them regardless of the personalities involved (Alderfer, 1987; Argyris, 1958; Emery, 1993; Lippitt and White, 1943; Lowin, 1958).

The role of organizational structure in dealing with environmental problems seems crucial because an appropriate organizational structure may provide the foundation for the creation, establishment, and institutionalization of the necessary conditions and mechanisms for the attainment of project objectives and the maintenance of their outcomes, while eliminating/reducing negative externalities. At the macro level, these mechanisms would rely on market-based environmental policies that assign legal and financial responsibilities to industries and individuals, better quantified cost/benefit analysis of project developments, and adequate monetizing of environmental goods and/or damages through environmental accounting, environmental adders, tradeable permits, eco-taxes and the like.

1.6 The Importance of Organizational Structure

Lippitt and White's (1943) seminal work on group climates demonstrated that all human organizations embody one of only two genotypic and fundamentally technical organizational structures: (1) Bureaucratic; and, (2) Participative Democratic. Emery (1993) refers to bureaucratic and participative democratic structures as the first and second design principles, respectively (Ibid). The bureaucratic, or First Design Principle (DP1), has a dominant hierarchy inhabited by specialized individuals with highly defined tasks. In this type of structure the redundancy, essential to the flexibility, adaptability, and viability of all systems is incorporated through the addition of redundant "parts" (i.e., individuals with the same skills) (Emery, 1993). This accounts for the technical name "redundancy of parts" (Emery, 1993). It has also been called "the Megamachine" (Mumford, 1967). The participative democratic, or Second Design Principle (DP2), has a non-dominant hierarchy or flat organizational structure inhabited by individuals who are highly specialized, but multi-skilled. In this type of structure, the redundancy, essential to the flexibility, adaptability, and viability of all systems, is incorporated through the process of multiskilling (i.e., individuals with different [but redundant] functions). This accounts for the technical name "redundancy of functions" (Emery, 1993). Organizational researchers have found that bureaucratic (DP1) and participative democratic (DP2) structures have profound and predictable effects on the people who live and work within them regardless of the personalities involved (Alderfer, 1987; Argyris, 1958; Emery, 1993; Lippitt and White, 1943; Lowin, 1958). The role of organizational structure in dealing with environmental problems seems crucial because an appropriate organizational structure may provide the foundation for the creation, establishment, and institutionalization of the necessary conditions and mechanisms for the attainment of project objectives and the maintenance of their outcomes, while eliminating/reducing negative externalities. At the macro level, these mechanisms would rely on market-based environmental policies that assign legal and financial responsibilities to industries and individuals, better quantified cost/benefit analysis of project developments, and adequate monetizing of environmental goods and/or damages through environmental accounting, environmental adders, tradeable permits, eco-taxes and the like (Atkins and Lowe, 1977; Connor et al., 1995; Costanza, 1990; Cropper and Oates, 1992; Howarth, 1996; Jordan, 1995; Maskin, 1994; Myles, 1995; Papandreou, 1994; Usher, 1992). At the micro level, the potential for the appropriate organizational structure to enhance project performance and eliminate (rather than just reduce or internalize) negative externalities needs to be examined.

1.6.1 Sustainable Development: a Utopian Scenario?

Definitions of sustainability abound. However, all definitions of "sustainability" seem to share at least two things in common: (1) they are all anthropocentric (unless the human component is removed from the picture); and, (2) they all speak of an ideal process or state. Based on the these two observations and on the seminal work of Ackoff and Emery (1972), the working definition of sustainability that is used throughout this research is: Sustainability: a socio-ecological process characterized by ideal-seeking behavior on the part of its human component. Ideal-seeking behavior, with regards to socio-ecological processes, means behavior characterized by the desire (i.e., system effectivity) and ability (i.e., environmental affordances such as, opportunity and resources): 1. to progress toward an ideal by choosing a new goal when one has been achieved (or the effort to achieve it has failed), and 2. to sacrifice a goal for the sake of an ideal. Only ideals serve as appropriate guidelines within a context of uncertainty and complexity because only ideals are time-free, hence, intrinsically adaptive in themselves (Emery, 1993). The four universal ideals are:(1) Homonomy; (2) Nurturance; (3) Humanity; and, (4) Beauty (Ibid). However, in order for ideal-seeking behavior to be manifested, the system (e.g., a person) must provide the effectivity (i.e., the desire) to behave as such, and the environment must provide the right affordances (i.e., opportunity and resources). 1.6.2 From Goal-seeking Organizations to Ideal-Seeking Systems Human behaviors (e.g., participation, commitment) and factors (e.g., values, institutions, policies) that influence and motivate those behaviors are central to any understanding of organizational performance. People's actions do not arise as simple responses to external or internal stimuli per se, but as a response to situations determined by the relationship between the effectivities of the system and the environmental affordances through positive and negative feedback loops (Emery, 1985). In other words, people's behaviors are determined by the relationship between the individual and his/her environment. Thus, negative behaviors (i.e., maladaptations, such as apathy, dissociation, lack of responsibility, commitment and participation) seem attributable to a specific organizational structure, or design principle, which restricts the effectivities of its elements within a turbulent environment. The restriction of element effectivities gives rise to goal-seeking or "rational" individualistic behaviors as a requirement for survival within this type of organizational structure and turbulent environment. On the other hand, positive behaviors, such as altruism, high responsibility, commitment and participation, seem attributable to a contrasting organizational structure, or design principle, which enhances the effectivities of its elements within this type of structure and turbulent environment. The enhancement of element effectivities gives rise to ideal-seeking behavior through the purposeful pursuit of ideals. Because ideal-seeking behavior and choice are intimately related (Ackoff & Emery, 1972), the future of human kind is increasingly determined by the choices people make and their behavior (Emery, 1985). Given the importance of organizational and/or institutional issues in terms of human behavior, and based on the working definition of sustainability used in this research, it seems only appropriate to focus on the importance of organizational design principles. 1.7 Research Hypotheses The hypotheses of this research state that: 21 projects with an organizational structure that more closely resembles a bureaucracy (DP1) reduce project performance, increase negative impacts, and do not allow for the sustainability of desired project outcomes. 22 projects with an organizational structure that more closely resembles a participative-democratic organizational structure (DP2) enhance project performance, reduce/eliminate negative impacts, and allow for the sustainability of desired outcomes. Hypothesis #2 is based on the assumption that, given the appropriate level of participation, fostered by a participative democratic organizational structure, people's actions and behaviors will be consistent (i.e., ideal-seeking) with the requirements for sustainable systems, that is, economic, social and environmental justice.

2. LITERATURE REVIEW

2.1 The Rhetoric of Sustainable Development

The fundamental rhetoric of "sustainable development" has always been economic. Economists are ubiquitous in development projects as a sort of chosen rational instrumentality of national progress (Bennett, 1988). This economic or "capitalistic" bias, depending on one's perspective, has several implications. The most severe and pervasive implication has been an economic theory which views humans as "rational" economic beings, i.e., homo economicus, or mere "profit-maximizing machines." From this view, it followed that, by promising maximum net economic gains people (e.g., participants or "beneficiaries") would accept any policy or be committed to the implementation and success of any project, thus, achieving a questionable atmosphere of certainty (Bennett, 1988). Does such a world exist? This view has been characterized as a radical and arguably dangerous abstraction from social reality (Daly and Cobb, 1989; Damasio, 1995; Ormerod, 1994; Soros, 1996).

2.2 Environmental Economics and Negative Externalities

Negative externalities is a central issue to environmental economics and sustainability. Unfortunately, economic models allow economists to ignore significant components of the real economy as "externalities" because these components are "external" to the exchange processes of the market. But externalities are not external to our biosphere and, thus, do not stay "external." The concept of externalities has been explicitly discussed since Alfred Marshall's (1890) Principles of Economics. Marshall introduced the notions of external economies and diseconomies. These notions evolved into pecuniary and technological externalities of production and consumption (Papandreou, 1994). Pecuniary externalities are not necessarily a sign of market failure and, thus, are not of much concern for policy. For instance, the diminished returns of existing firms caused by the entry into the market of a new firm, or the expansion of an industry, driving up the labor price to another firm are examples of the market reallocating resources to the highest value uses and, eventually, private marginal costs and benefits should, according to economic theory, equate. By contrast, technological externalities deal not only with the efficient use of resources but also with their efficient and equitable allocation. They represent third party effects on production possibilities or utility levels. The classic example is pollution (Papandreou, 1995).

2.2.1 Global View of Negative Externalities

At the international level, aid agencies, such as the United States Agency for International Development (USAID), the World Bank, the United Nations Environment Programme (UNEP), and the World Resources Institute (WRI) have demonstrated concern for uncompensated effects, or negative externalities, associated with development projects such as pollution and environmental degradation. These not only are seen as a great waste of resources but also as a major threat for global stability and sustainable development. So long as social costs are ignored, the gap between the haves and have-nots will continue to widen, at the expense of the environment(Cocks and Walker, 1994; UNEP, 1995; von Amsberg, 1993; Wichterman, 1995; WRI, 1993).

2.2.2 Local View of Negative Externalities

In developing countries, mechanisms to internalize, reduce, or eliminate negative externalities are either lacking, wrongfully implemented, or not implemented at all. This is particularly true in Ecuador, where the inefficient use and allocation of resources has led to decreased social welfare and to the deterioration of the social fabric (Southgate & Whitaker, 1994).

2.3 Possible Ways of Addressing the Negative Externalities Problem

To date, research on the issue has identified five basic ways to address the negative externalities problem: 1. Quality Control. 2. Taxes and Subsidies 3. Market Creation 4. Externality Internalization 5. Avoiding the Creation of Externalities.

1) Quality Control

This is the most common approach used throughout the world. It is a typical command-and-control approach forcing technology (e.g., ISO 9000, 14001, SA 8000). It is the most difficult to enforce and least efficient of all five options (McMorran and Nellor, 1994). This approach does not achieve the reduction of externalities at least cost and may even create barriers to entry and price increases (Papandreou, 1995).

2) Taxes and Subsidies

Environment or Pigouvian taxes have been used in a still unsuccessful attempt to bring social and private costs together. While "green" taxes can correct behavior and collect money (at least in theory), the externality problem has two sides and control by one side may not be efficient (e.g., airport and noise). In addition, determining the right amount of the tax is very difficult in the real world. An inappropriate tax could lead to inefficiently high costs (i.e., over abatement or under adjustment) (Papandreou, 1995). This is linked to the argument that imposing a Pigouvian tax on a monopolist could reduce rather than enhance social welfare (Cropper and Oates, 1992). Pigouvian taxes or subsidies are difficult to implement and introduce particularly for their implications for other policy objectives and thus encounter great opposition (McMorran and Nellor, 1994). Eco-taxes continue the perception that the environment is a liability on the balance sheet environment (Daly, 1996; Spires, 1996). However, given the little understanding of other alternatives, taxes will continue to be politically more feasible (Spires, 1996).

3) Market Creation

Market creation (i.e, quotas or tradable permits to existing firms) has been a preferred mechanism over Pigouvian taxes by most industrialized countries. Market creation is slowly growing but is far from becoming the norm. While this mechanism permits, in theory, the achievement of environmental goals at a minimum economic cost, it is difficult to determine the right amount of permits to be issued. It can also be viewed as sanctioning the negative externality (Cropper and Oates, 1992; Daly, 1996).

4) Externality Internalization

Externality internalization, i.e., the victim and the perpetrator negotiate to efficiency. The government role is limited to ensuring that no monopoly power is exerted or that no free-riding on the negotiation takes place. The main barrier to this approach are the institutionalized organizational structures in place. Within this type of institutionalized organizational environments (i.e., rigid dominant hierarchies), where lack of accountability, poorly defined and unenforceable property rights and regulations prevail, it is counter to the individual interest to cooperate, creating high transaction costs and evasive strategies by perpetrators (Vasquez, 1997).

5) Avoiding the Creation of Externalities

This fifth alternative has remained mostly theoretical. Avoiding the creation of a negative externality could only be achieved if, first of all, the potential "perpetrator" of the negative externality is aware of the potential externality and has a viable alternative that would avoid its creation. If there is no viable alternative in place, one must be created. This is what matching system effectivities and environmental affordances is about. Matching System Effectivities and Environmental Affordances The matching of systems' effectivities to environmental affordances could only take place in an organizational structure conducive to such matching by use of timely feedback and continuous conscious, conceptual and experiential learning (Katz and Kahn, 1966). In a framework for ecological learning (i.e., open system) system and environment are interdependent. They are mutually affecting as explained by the model of directive correlations (Sommerhoff, 1974). Given the correlation between system and environment it is essential for any one system to match its effectivities to the affordances of its environment if the system is to be actively adaptive, i.e., purposeful (Emery, 1985). An environment containing two parties in potential conflict does not afford the parties the effectivity of cooperation in the absence of a mediating affordance. It does afford, however, the opportunity for a confrontation. Environmental affordances can only be specified with respect to a system's effectivities. System effectivities can only be specified with respect to environmental affordances (Ibid). The conceptualization of the relation between system and environment allows for a more precise analysis of organizational structures and is summarized by Emery F. (1985) as follows:

1. People's actions arise in response to the situation defined by the relations between their effectivities and the environmental affordances.

2. The interrelation of affordances and effectivities must be explicitly dealt with in any model of communication attempting to explain human actions.

3. Communication facilitates organized activities and the matching of effectivities to affordances.

4. Organizations are nothing more than controlled and coordinated effectivities of coactors.

The need to align organizational systems and processes (i.e., system effectivities) with natural processes and the environment (i.e., environmental affordances) is also recognized and outlined in Westley and Vredenburg's (1996) argument concerning what they call "Technospheres" and "Ecospheres." A Modified Coasian Approach The idea of designing for "fit" or sustainability is not new and is congruent with the Coasian argument (Korten, 1980). That argument states that in the absence of transaction costs and strategic behavior (e.g., monopolies), distortions associated with externalities will be resolved through voluntary bargaining among the parties involved, and that no further inducements (e.g., Pigouvian taxes) would be needed in order to achieve a Pareto efficient outcome (Cropper and Oates, 1992). Research based on a modified Coasian stance has demonstrated that cooperation, through contractual agreements, suffices to achieve efficiency as long as there is no monopoly power and the externalities involved are excludable, i.e., do not allow free-riding. Otherwise, government intervention will be needed to avoid free-riding on the agreements (Maskin, 1994).

Externality internalization and avoiding the creation of externalities to begin with through a modified Coasian approach (i.e., matching of system effectivities and environmental affordances) could be, under a participative and cooperative scenario, not only the most common sense approach, but also the most efficient of all in terms of Pareto optimality . However, a modified Coasian approach (i.e., a cooperative-bargaining process) could only be productively undertaken within an organizational design where timely feedback is possible, transaction costs are low, and where it is in the individual interest to cooperate (Emery, 1993, 1995; Stacey, 1995).

2.4 The Record of Major Development Institutions

Inefficient use and allocation of resources are associated with both developing and developed economies and institutions where the mechanisms to deal with negative externalities are minimal, if any, and where the appropriate organizational structure is non-existent (Costanza, 1990; Cropper and Oates, 1992; Maskin, 1994; Southgate and Whitaker, 1994; Templet, 1995).

2.4.1 The World Bank

The World Bank has been under global scrutiny regarding its lending practices and the global implications of its funded projects. It has launched, during the past few years, a global campaign to convince people about the "greenness" of its lending practices. The overall impact of the World Bank, since its establishment in 1944 to promote self-sustaining economic development, has been characterized as, on balance, a failure (Osterfeld, 1994). Because the repayment of World Bank loans is guaranteed by recipient governments, there is no accountability to worry about when conducting a feasibility analysis of projects to be funded (Ibid). It is also argued that the organizational structure of the World Bank does not allow for an active-adaptive relationship of the peoples involved/affected by a project and their environment (Kerr and Sanghi, 1992). World Bank projects have yet to be based on concepts of open and evolving systems built on participative-democratic principles of experiential learning and contextualism (Allen, et al., 1996; Emery, 1981). The type of failure referred to in the United Nations report (UNEP, 1995) is starkly evident in Kottak's (1985) analysis of 82 World Bank-financed projects. Kottak analyzed the role played by socio-cultural variables and their contribution to the design of Bank-assisted rural development projects. He found that greater economic returns, in some cases twice as high, were associated with what he calls "enhanced sociocultural fit," meaning that the projects acknowledged established socioeconomic and cultural patterns, which allowed for the incorporation of these variables into project design (Kottak, 1985). In a comparison of rates of return for projects, Kottak found that socioculturally compatible projects had an average rate of return of 18.3 percent. Socioculturally incompatible projects had less than half that, at 8.6 percent (Ibid). Socioculturally compatible projects incorporated indigenous cultural practices and social structures in project implementation. This allowed for the elimination of uncompensated effects which could explain the difference in the rate of return. This difference in return on investment is a tax (i.e., a technological negative externality) borne by the people. The majority of the reports examined by Kottak pointed to problems that arose because during project preparation or design, socioeconomic information was either lacking, insufficiently analyzed, or simply ignored (lack of accountability or a pretense of knowledge?). Kottak's analysis stresses the importance of proper design as a key ingredient in project success. He considers putting first those who must live with the results as critical, for they, those who must live with the results, become the project's best monitoring and evaluation team (Kottak, 1985). While Kottak acknowledges that assessing cultural compatibility as an ex post exercise is a judgmental endeavor, he argues for the value, not of precise percentages, but of identifying mechanisms through which a better compatibility, or social fit, can be routinely incorporated into project development (Kottak, 1985).

2.4.2 The USAID Record

A review, by Wichterman (1995), of USAID-supported development programs, shows that few projects emphasized sustainability as a major goal. This review also showed that few projects demonstrated an understanding of sustainability, at both the theoretical and practical levels during the project design phase. Few USAID projects are monitored and evaluated to ascertain whether benefit flows are sustainable (Wichterman, 1995). Wichterman also indicates that a study [IRIS, 1994] found that, overall, less than 8 of 44 projects USAID considered to be "successful" had a high probability of achieving benefit sustainability (Wichterman, 1995). It has been argued that the little emphasis given to sustainability in AID projects is due to a lack of understanding of what sustainability is all about (Finsterbush and Van Wicklin, 1987;

Hudson, 1991; Wichterman, 1995). 2.5 Project Failures: Unsustainable by Design? The little attention given to sustainability in AID projects may be due to a lack of understanding of how to achieve sustainability rather than to a lack of understanding of its meaning or significance. As was noted earlier in reference to USAID SO4, people (the target population, project team, government entities) are often at the core of project failure. There is evidence to suggest that this is an issue that can be characterized as a design flaw (Bennet, 1988; Finsterbush and Van Wicklin, 1987; Hudson, 1991; Narayan, 1995). Programs developed at a distance, with little or no compatibility with, or reference to, the perceptions and capacities of local peoples have often failed (UNEP, 1995). Since the late seventies, the concept of compatibility, or "fit," has assumed a central role in the fields of business policy and organizational design. Research has shown the importance of the relationships amongst task, environment, and organizational variables (Ackoff & Emery, 1972; Emery, 1993; Korten, 1980). The general conclusion of this research is that the performance of an organization is a function of the fit achieved amongst the variables involved (Korten, 1980). Livestock Projects (East Africa) The East African livestock projects surveyed by Bennett (1988) may epitomize unsuccessful development programs. Bennett's survey of project papers, from USAID and the World Bank, of all the East African livestock projects in the 1970s found that no project had attained its predicted goals (Bennett, 1988). The reasons for these negative results, according to Bennett, point to extraneous factors such as social organization, status differentials, authority, and cultural customs. These factors can be summarized as a socio-cultural misfit or design problems. These design problems seem to have kept the people affected by the projects as subjects of fate unable to become shapers of their own future for they had no say, much less control, over the projects' decision-making processes (Ibid). The design of these pastoral development projects in Africa exemplifies Schneider's (1988) work on the "Principles of Development." Schneider refers to the reports, from the Harper's Ferry workshop on pastoral programs in Africa where, after 20 years and over $600 million, no pastoral program had been a success. Schneider considers the imposition of western-style ranching schemes on pastoral people as the main explanation for the failures. He indicates that no one involved in the livestock projects bothered to ask the pastoralists about the appropriateness of the ranching schemes to be implemented, assuming that their scientific and expert knowledge would suffice to make their blue-print project work. This assumption eliminated, from the very beginning, any possibility for internalizing any foreseeable negative externality. Soil and Water Conservation Projects (World-wide) One of the most comprehensive studies ever carried out to assess the commonalities of poor performance projects was conducted by Hudson (1991). Hudson reviewed 1,441 soil conservation development projects with the purpose of identifying the reasons for success or failure. According to Hudson, the most significant conclusion from the study was the importance of project design. In one third of all cases, poor design was the most important factor leading to poor performance and uncompensated effects. Overall, 86 percent of poor performance projects had design problems. He did not find any significant correlation between project budget and performance (Hudson, 1991).The strong positive correlation between project success/failure and the scores obtained from appraisal and design, reinforces the conclusion from the World

Bank report (1985) about the importance of project design for success. Development Projects (World-wide) Finsterbush and Van Wicklin (1987) analyzed 52 USAID Impact Evaluation Reports on development projects carried out throughout the world. The authors indicate that they found numerous examples of successful and unsuccessful participation across the 52 cases. They studied the correlations of 15 "participation" variables with project effectiveness. They found the variables, adequacy of communication and beneficiary commitment, strongly correlated ($r=0.75$ and 0.67, respectively) with project performance at every level (i.e., design, implementation, and maintenance of project outcomes). They also found the variables, increased community capacity and local control, and ownership of project outputs, significantly correlated ($r=0.50$ and 0.44, respectively) with project effectiveness (Ibid). The study specifically refers to five cases (i.e., rural education in Paraguay, self-housing in Panama, potable water in Tunisia, agricultural research in Thailand, and water supplies in Peru) where they found that participation, its absence or misuse, was the most important factor in contributing to project success or failure (Ibid). Finally, they also found that beneficiary project relations (i.e., adequacy of communication with beneficiaries, beneficiary commitment, and ownership of project outputs) were crucial for project success (Finsterbush and Van Wicklin, 1987). Water Projects (World-wide) In an attempt to provide scientific quantitative evidence of the efficacy of participation in determining project effectiveness, relative to other factors, Narayan (1995) conducted a study based on multivariate analyses of data derived from evaluation reports of 121 rural water projects implemented by different agencies around the world. The project reports were supplemented by in-depth anthropological and sociological studies (Ibid). This study, specifically addressed, inter alia, the following questions: 1. Does people participation contribute to project effectiveness? 2. How important is this contribution relative to other factors? 3. What factors and strategies influence participation in collective action? 4. What are the implications for policy reform? The author concluded that the two main illustrations that emerged from the study are: (1) Beneficiary participation is critical for achieving project effectiveness and building local capacity; and (2) Rural water projects have to be fundamentally redesigned to incorporate beneficiary participation (Narayan, 1995). Participation contributed significantly to overall project effectiveness, i.e., higher proportion of water systems in good condition, greater overall economic benefits, higher percentages of target population reached, and greater environmental benefits, even after controlling for 18 direct and indirect determinants of outcomes (Ibid). Narayan examined how final outcomes were affected by the quality of outcomes at the design, implementation, construction, and maintenance stages, finding that participation was the single most important determinant of overall quality implementation and that the impact throughout the project cycle was significantly greater than it was during a single stage (Ibid). Narayan also found that local control and ownership were significantly correlated to overall participation ($r=0.79$). Other statistically significant factors found to strongly influence beneficiary participation were: (1) demand for the services the project is supposed to deliver; (2) organization of beneficiaries; and (3) autonomy and client-orientation of the implementing agency (Ibid). 2.6 Project Success: Sustainable by Design? COMUNIDEC (The Andes) After three decades of development aid throughout the

Andean region, a process designed and managed by the beneficiary participants themselves has become evident (COMUNIDEC, 1993; Ramón, 1995). This process has allowed for the development of "Diagnósticos Rurales Rápidos" (Rapid Rural Appraisals or RRA). RRA allow for better and faster acquisition of information and at a lower cost than conventional methods previously used (Ibid). RRA evolved to give rise to the "Diagnósticos Rurales Participativos" (Participatory Rural Appraisals or PRA). PRA aim at the training of the rural peoples so that they themselves do their own planning and become the owners of the results and consequences. With this new tool, and the support of the Fundación Interamericana (Interamerican Foundation) and the World Resources Institute (WRI), the "Planeamiento Andino Comunitario" (Community Andean Planning or CAP) came into being. The CAP is a participative and essentially democratic methodology that has allowed Andean communities to organize themselves to plan and direct their future in a given time frame (COMUNIDEC, 1993; Ramón, 1995). A key commonality in the success of 59 projects followed by COMUNIDEC between 1985 and 1992 has been their participative organizational structure. This participative structure is an overt design feature of the projects. It shows the great capacity, honesty and efficiency with which, given the right organizational environment, communities can conceive, design, and implement their own projects. The approach to project design followed by these communities allowed their members to behave as purposeful individuals in search of an active-adaptive relationship with their environments. The Community Baboon Sanctuary (Belize) Elsewhere, much work has been done, and continues to be done, in an attempt to achieve and maintain project benefits. A case in point is the

Community Baboon Sanctuary (CBS) in Belize. The CBS began as an experiment to increase the population of black howler monkeys on private lands with very limited socioeconomic incentives (Hartup, 1994). The CBS project managed to achieve and maintain its objective i.e., to increase the monkey population (as of 1994). The driving force behind the apparent success of this program, as suggested by Hartup, was the commitment and active participation of the community voluntarily involved (Ibid). Given the voluntary nature of the CBS, people organized themselves in a participative and essentially democratic manner, taking ownership of the project. This approach allowed community members to become responsible and accountable for the success of the project motivated by the benefits associated therewith. The Catchment Approach (Kenya) The Catchment Approach to Soil and Water Conservation and Agricultural Regeneration in Kenya began in 1988, after 50 years of only "patchy" and "unsustainable" soil and water conservation programs (Pretty et al., 1995). In 1988, the Ministry of Agriculture considered that the only possibility to achieve widespread conservation coverage was to get people to embrace soil and water-conserving practices on their own terms (Ibid). The Catchment Approach became interdisciplinary and community mobilizing. Catchment committees articulated local priorities and provided a link with external agencies, thus maintaining a sense of ownership, cooperation, and accountability. The concept of the Catchment Approach evolved primarily due to the introduction of participatory methods which got the communities involved in the analysis of their own farming and conservation problems. Decisions and recommendations were made with the active participation of the community members (Pretty et al., 1995).

This approach enabled them, not only to eliminate negative externalities, but also to generate positive ones by drawing the active participation of neighboring communities. The authors also indicate that a self-evaluation conducted in six districts found the most significant impact where there had been "interactive participation." For them, this meant that people participated in joint analysis leading to action plans and the formation of new local institutions, or the strengthening of existing ones. This approach involved interdisciplinary methodologies that sought multiple perspectives and allowed groups to take control over local decisions. This created and maintained a cooperative environment with a sense of ownership and accountability for the projects in the community, thus, giving them a stake in maintaining those structures or practices (Ibid). In participating communities, crop yields were increasing; farmers were growing a greater diversity of crops; there were more trees and ground cover; groundwater resources were being recharged; land prices and labor rates were increasing; and communities were actively replicating successes to neighboring communities (Pretty et al., 1995). The organizational structure of the Kenya project was participative, cooperative, and bottom-up. Committees articulated local priorities by means of an interactive participation, thus providing a link with external agencies. This interactive participation, which created, maintained and strengthened a sense of ownership, cooperation, and project accountability, proved critical for the success of the project and the elimination of negative externalities (Ibid). The KASHA Project (Botswana) The KASHA (Kang Self Help Association) project in the village of Kang, in Botswana, is yet another example that demonstrates the efficiency of local efforts at sustainability when these efforts combine resource considerations with human needs (Ameyaw, 1992). The KASHA project managed to build a resource center, to develop skill training programs, to implement conservation programs, and to improve the town of Kang. The framework for the KASHA's development initiatives were based on motivational and sustaining factors and strategies. The motivational factors were community self-reliance and responsibility, economic security and social mobilization. Some of the sustaining factors were strong dedicated leadership by women, openness of the Association to all Kang citizens, shared power and administrative duties, spatial linkages, local resources and initiatives, locally designed projects managed by local members, and shared communal values. Some of the strategies developed were the formation of KASHA Resource Center, capacity building, weekend learning programs, local mobilization, skills training, outreach program, and self-reliance (Ibid). A Hospital Experimental Study (USA) Another successful project, albeit in a highly "developed" context, where the key aspect for its success was its organizational structure, is the experimental study conducted in a hospital by Bragg and Andrews (1973). Based on Lowin's (1968) theoretical model of Participative Decision Making (PDM), whereby the decisions as to the activities that must be done are made by the very persons who are to execute those decisions, Bragg and Andrews hypothesized that, by creating a participative decision-making environment, employees' attitudes would improve, i.e., absenteeism would decline, and productivity would increase. The results of their 18 month experimental study indicated that after PDM was introduced into a hospital laundry department, employees' attitudes statistically improved, i.e., absence rates declined, and productivity increased. The control groups showed no improvement. The authors indicate that the performance differences between the experimental and comparison groups were statistically and practically significant (Bragg and Andrews, 1973). Participatory Research in United States Sustainable Agriculture (USSA) Dlott et al. (1994) present a case study in insect pest management where Rapid Rural Appraisal (RRA) methods were adapted to fit local circumstances of the California Clean Growers Association (a US peach production farmer organization) to develop a research agenda. Farmer participation in sustainable agricultural research in the United States, according to Dlott et al. (1994), has been "meager" compared to that of the "Third World." According to the authors, farmer participation in the United States has been mostly philosophical and/or theoretical. The authors indicate that use of "participatory" research strategies in USSA will require facing philosophical and methodological monoisms at the individual and institutional levels. The authors further indicate that the case study demonstrated that participatory research strategies provide effective approaches for the design and conduct of sustainable agricultural research and that farmer participation contributed with essential knowledge for the provision of relevant information (Dlott et al., 1994). 2.7 Conclusions and Lessons from Projects Reviewed The consistent theme common to both project failures and successes is organizational structure with concomitant behaviors associated with a particular organizational structure. The review of the literature on development outcomes correlates project effectiveness (success in meeting project objectives) with project structures that incorporate a specific type of beneficiary participation in design and implementation. The same literature associates negative outcomes (failure to meet project objectives, misallocation of resources and externalities) with a contrasting organizational structure that incorporates other types of beneficiary participation. Although "participation" throughout the reviewed literature of development projects takes on different colorings, it still remains as a process of human interactions. The environment (e.g., bureaucratic vs. participative-democratic) within which these human interactions take place seems crucial. The literature reviewed directly points towards bureaucratic, highly hierarchical, and non-cooperative organizational structures as the most significant underlying aspect common to all unsuccessful development projects (Bennett, 1988; Hudson, 1991; Kottak, 1985; Pretty et al., 1996; Wichterman, 1995). An organizational structure, or project design, that generates a cooperative and learning environment conducive to effective participation, commitment, and active adaptation is seen as critical and common to the successful projects (Ameyaw, 1992; COMUNIDEC, 1993; Finsterbush and Van Wicklin, 1987; Isham et at., 1995; Kottak, 1985; Narayan, 1995; Pretty et al.,1995; Ramón, 1995). The project failures and successes reviewed here were not inherent to specific regions or communities. Nor were they due to financial constraints, poor science or technology, or environmental circumstances. These failures and successes do seem to have been consistently associated with organizational or institutional structures which can be categorized as either bureaucratic or participative democratic. However, this clear dichotomy is only possible in theory. In practice, organizational structures range from those which more closely resemble bureaucratic organizations to those which more closely resemble participative democratic organizations.

3. What is there to learn about organizational design?

3.1 The Anachronistic Bureaucratic Mindset

Bureaucracies seem destined to be forever in conflict with human values, individual fulfilment and social equality (Kranz, 1976). About a hundred years ago the word bureaucracy meant something good (to some, it still does). It had the connotation of a "rational" and "efficient" approach to organizing something, bringing the same logic to government and institutional work as the assembly lines brought to factories (Bjerknes, 1993). The explanation for these positive connotations is given by Max Weber's view of bureaucracy not only as the most efficient instrument of large-scale administration ever developed but also as the triumph of capitalism over feudal management designs (Weber, 1947). The positive connotations of bureaucracy are also explained by the environment of a time which, according to Emery and Trist's taxonomy (1965), was disturbed and reactive (Type III), not turbulent (Type IV). Within this Type III environment, where labor was cheap, plentiful, and largely unskilled, a dominant hierarchy based on redundant "parts" was probably the best means of creating a "reliable" system from cheap and unreliable parts (Emery, 1993). Bureaucracy, as a system of administration, was seen as a particular feature of Western society related to its growing complexity (Weber, 1947). It was rooted to the so-called "social contract," whereby individuals accepted a common superior power to protect them from their own ignorance (Hobbes, 1651). The French sociologist, Emile Durkheim (1984), saw societies in terms of the division of labor within them. In primitive societies there is relatively little division of labor, and that which does exist is largely based on age and sex. But, as societies become more complex, their members no longer share the same experiences, and, thus, a new basis of uniting individuals (or personal goals) with the collectivity (or common ideals) is required. Durkheim characterized modern society as based on "organic solidarity", (i.e., the division of labor) in contrast to primitive societies based mostly on "mechanical solidarity" (i.e., the collective consciousness) (Ibid). Durkheim's organic and the mechanical solidarity concepts are both based on a closed-system perspective.

3.2 Defining Bureaucracy

Some of the key attributes of bureaucracy according to Weber (1947) are: 1. Rational calculability of decision making (i.e., decisions as logical consequences of the rule of law) 2. Concentration of means of administration 13 Enduring (indestructible or relatively permanent) structure of authority relations Max Weber introduced and idealized the term bureaucracy in the beginning of the 19th century. His view of bureaucracy, as a post-Marxian theorist, was composite of an "administrative hierarchy" and an organization of professional services (Weber, 1947). Weber's concept of bureaucracy was a rather utopian one which included the following characteristics: (1) a hierarchy of authority with powers and responsibilities understood by all; (2) a clear-cut division of labor among officials; (3) recruitment of officials on the basis of their technical knowledge and expertise; (4) an explicit set of rules for making decisions; (5) a strict separation of official business from personal concerns; and (6) the establishment of a career service. These characteristics, supposedly, made bureaucracy the most efficient method of coordinating and accomplishing any task. Thus, Weber viewed bureaucracy as a system of law where leaders obtain their offices through legal procedures and the power to rule was vested in their positions rather than in themselves as individuals (Ibid). The emergence of bureaucracy, as we know it, can be traced back to the end of the 17th century with the advent of world economy and resources competition (Emery, 1977). By the end of the 18th century, when large organizational acquisitions took place (triggered by technological breakthroughs in the energy generation and communications field), bureaucracy was fully developed, and its institutionalization, with its hierarchies of personal dominance, began (Emery, 1977; Hyneman, 1950; Kranz, 1976). Bureaucracy, a structure that was initially created to perform a facilitating task for a larger structure, ended up securing its own survival as its primary aim (Beer, 1972). Regardless of its definition, bureaucracy is viewed by people in general, and most organization theorists in particular, as the only existing genotypic structure and, thus, for all practical purposes, as the only possible form of organizing anything. This view is what Michel Resnick (1996) calls "the centralized mindset." Given this mindset, whereby the only possible way of genotypic organizational structure is given and fixed, the efforts of organization theorists and consultants have revolved around the phenotypic (or external) characteristics of bureaucratic structures. This is best illustrated by the continuous emergence of new types, or phenotypic disguises, of organizations. Literature advocating a variety of organizational (re)designs, such as "Poised," "Fractal," "Organic," "Learning," "Knowing," "Chaordic," abounds, as also abound "participatory" forms of decision-making (Alutto and Belasco, 1972; Argyris, 1955; Bragg and Andrews, 1973; Fallon, 1974; Fitzgerald, 1997; Gormley, 1989; Hirsch and Shulman, 1976; Packard, 1989; Pretty et al., 1996; Ramsdell, 1994; Resnick and Patti, 1980; Thrupp et al., 1994; Toch and Grant, 1982; Turner, 1991; Wynn, 1995). These organizational (re)design efforts leave the genotypic (structural) design unquestioned and unchanged. Concomitantly, efforts to increase participatory decision-making have remained phenotypic (superficial) as opposed to genotypic or systemic. In alleging to effect change, most organizational theorists and consultants simply (re)dress the phenotypic organizational structure. Thus, initial positive changes, such as increased participation due to an "invigorating" leadership workshop, soon dwindle down as things go back to the normal maladaptations (e.g., apathy, lack of responsibility, low/no commitment). The "genotypic" view of bureaucracy, as opposed to a "phenotypic" one, is of paramount importance and pivotal to the proposition presented here. It is known from biology that phenotype is determined by genotype and not the other way around. It follows, then, that no internal or "genotypic" re-structuring of an organization will ever be possible by re-designing its "phenotypic" or external structure. 3.2.1 Explaining the Anachronic Pervasiveness of Bureaucracy The bureaucratic pervasiveness could be readily explained by at least three centuries of instilling in the Western management mindset the concept of centralized authority and the root metaphor of the machine. Thus giving rise to " the centralized mindset" (Resnick, 1996) and its fixation on the Cartesian, mechanistic, view of the universe (Pepper, 1942). However, the most pragmatic explanation for the pervasiveness of bureaucracy is given by Emery and Trist's (1965) seminal work on the causal texture of organizational environments. The causal texture of the environment at the beginning of the Industrial Revolution was, according to Emery and Trist, disturbed and reactive (Type III). At that time, individual "parts" were cheap and plentiful (this is still true today in many parts of the world such as China, which has encouraged the relocation of many manufacturing jobs) and the lead times for organizations to learn new modes of response were long (Emery, 1977). This is certainly not the case in today's world. The disturbed and reactive causal texture of the Type III environment (characterized by competition) required reliable (fool-proof) structures in order to compete and stay in business (Emery, 1993). Within this Type III environment, the best way to create a reliable organizational structure from unskilled and "unreliable" parts was through redundant "parts" and strict hierarchies of control and supervision. This gave rise to the institutionalization of hierarchies of personal dominance (Ibid). Once the bureaucratic design had been chosen by those in control or in power and imposed on the rest, every effort was made to keep the cost of individual parts down, e.g., by accessing pools of poor and dispossessed unemployed through maquiladoras and "sweat-shops" and by job specializing, standardizing, and downsizing so as to minimize training and operation costs. For Boje, Gephart, & Thatchenkery (1996), the pervasiveness of bureaucracy could also be explained by the view of "modern bureaucracy" as technically superior to all other forms of organization because "bureaucratic officials were supposed to execute tasks based only on impersonal rules and their technical knowledge and expertise" (Boje et al., 1996:27). In contrast to pre-modern forms of bureaucracy, which were based on traditional authority under patrimonial rule, modern bureaucracies were characterized, inter alia, by "rational"/legal authority, rules and regulations, specialization and delimitation of work activities, and a strict hierarchy of authority. The technical rationality premises of modern bureaucracy, however, were rapidly replaced by premises based on social Darwinism (Boje et al., 1996). Max Weber, who regarded bureaucracy as technically superior (at least in theory) to any other form of organization (Reinhard, 1962), did warn us of the alienating forces of bureaucracy and its potential to turn into an "iron cage" for modern consciousness (Weber, 1947). He supplied also one of the keys to the historical development of bureaucracy by seeing it as characteristic of the movement from social anarchy toward rational social organization in modern societies with governments based on a system of law where leaders obtain their offices through legal procedures, and the power to rule is vested in their positions rather than in feudal practices of inherited or purchased positions (Ibid.). Finally, the ubiquity of bureaucracy can also be explained by the "legitimization" or "indoctrination" of the bureaucratic structure in the 1900s through Theory X and Taylorism. Theory X and Taylorism view humans as machines to be fully exploited (Carnevale, 1995). However, the bureaucratic structure became an anachronism when our environment was no longer a Type III (i.e., disturbed and reactive) but Type IV (i.e., turbulent).

3.3 Organizations in a Turbulent and Increasingly Complex Environment

Most of the world inhabitants now live in a Type IV or turbulent environment. This environment is characterized by constant and sudden changes and demands a decentralized and enabling organizational structure, i.e., a structure where the responsibility for control and coordination of work remains with those doing the work, because decisions about the work being done need to be made most efficiently and effectively and no one knows better about the work being done than those who are actually doing it. Although the need to create an organizational structure conducive to high performance and sustainable outcomes has never been greater, there is little knowledge about how to design such organization (Bathrick, 1997; Emery, 1993; Resnick, 1997). The implication is that this need can only be fulfilled by changing the way organizations are genotypically (not just phenotypically) structured and designed. However, a genotypic organizational change can only take place if those in charge (e.g., organization theorists, consultants) have a conceptual knowledge and understanding of the existing and possible organizational design principles at the systemic or genotypic level. In a turbulent environment, one might reasonably expect to find that an analysis of constraints confronting most organizations is characterized as institutional (or organizational) as opposed to technical. People, their attitudes, and how they relate to each other (their organization), are the key to the success or failure of a collective endeavor in the dynamic and turbulent environment (Type IV) in which they live. This environment calls for an active-adaptive, and genotypically participative, organizational structure. Genotypic participation is used throughout this paper as genuine structural participation as opposed to phenotypic or pseudo types of participation .

3.4 Project Participation (Goal-seeking vs. Ideal-seeking) and Performance

A common understanding of what participation really means, or what a genotypically participatory organizational structure looks like, is required in order to have a general sense of what to do to design such an organization and how to implement its design (Finsterbush and Van Wicklin, 1987; Pretty et al., 1995). The history of US foreign aid legislation indicates a growing awareness of the concept of participation in AID development projects, especially after title IX of the Foreign

Assistance Act of 1966. This Act called upon AID to ensure
the maximum participation of the peoples of developing
countries through democratic initiatives (Finsterbush and Van
Wicklin, 1987). By the mid 1970s, beneficiary participation
had become part of the conventional rhetoric if not wisdom
(Ibid). Although different terms are used throughout the
literature of development projects (e.g., "socio-cultural fit,"
"appropriateness of design", "adequacy of communication",
"beneficiary commitment") they all point to the participation
of those for whom the project is being developed and the
organizational structure which at the end will determine the
"type" and degree of participation (Kottak, 1985; Hudson,
1991; Isham, et al., 1995; Pretty, et al., 1995). Definitions of
participation include, to a greater or lesser degree, a notion of
power and control in decision-making processes (Narayan,
1995; Pretty, 1994). Today, "beneficiary participation" has
become part of the vernacular in development efforts. Most of
the development initiatives, while incorporating beneficiary
"participation", have only changed the phenotype of
development efforts (evidenced by "new and improved
participative" projects), leaving their genotype (i.e.,
bureaucratic design principle) unquestioned and unchanged
(Bentley, 1994). Some development efforts employing
"participatory" methods may even look democratic on the
surface. But their bureaucratic characteristics remain virtually
untouched and unquestioned. Regardless of many efforts
around the world to incorporate "beneficiary participation" in
decision-making and control, the dominant paradigm of
development efforts remains bureaucratic (Thrupp et al.,
1994). Some still consider participation simply as a "tool" or a
"means" (Locke, 1986; Narayan, 1995); while others view it
as an end in and of itself (Carmen, 1990; Pretty, 1994). The

increased performance benefits of participatively designed work are consequences derived from this end (Barzelay, 1992; Bragg and Andrews, 1973; Cabaña, 1995; Fallon, 1974; Sashkin, 1986). Advocates of increased participation of the peoples affected in the organizational decision-making process name benefits characteristic of participative project structures as follows : 1. Increased data for informed decisions by organizational leaders 2. Increased individual and organizational responsibility, cooperation, and accountability 3. Increased organizational access to peoples' expertise, initiative, judgement, and commitment 4. Increased productivity and quality of product or service 5. Increased morale and job satisfaction 6. Increased motivation and commitment to organization decisions 7. Reduced stress and turnover rates (Ramsdell, 1994; Sashkin, 1986) A genotypically participative organizational structure is needed to adequately deal with the ever-greater relevant uncertainties of our turbulent environment (Emery, 1993). Unfortunately, efforts to investigate this issue commensurate with its importance have not yet taken place. The reasons for not doing so, at least in Organization Theory, may relate to lack of conceptual clarity (over-reliance on linear-thinking such as "scientific management" in a non-linear environment), inadvertent (or deliberate) neglect of, and misinterpretation of, Fred Emery's work (Boje, 1997), unfamiliarity with open systems theory, and to the relative ease of searching for technical solutions. Technical solutions, however, such as deterministic linear thinking and mechanistic ceteris-paribus problem-solving approaches, that attempt to solve a problem by holding uncontrollable variables constant, can no longer deal effectively (i.e., do not allow for active adaptation) with the increasing relevant uncertainties of our times. These technical solutions must be replaced by contextualistic puzzle-solving and non-linear thinking approaches, i.e., approaches that view a problem in its context as experienced, and not artificially abstracted from reality. Contextualistic puzzle-solving approaches that allow for continuous, conscious, conceptual, and experiential learning and, hence, active adaptation cannot be successfully undertaken within bureaucratic environments (Emery, M., 1997).

3.4.1 Defining the Term "Participation"

The meaning of participation has broadened along with its growing recognition and nominal importance. The words "participatory" or "participation" have application from meaning a simple consultation process for data collection to empowerment and capacity-building in attempts to justify the extension of state control and external decisions (Pretty et al., 1995). Participation can range from a mere presentation of an opinion, where the locus of authority lies elsewhere, to membership in the group that exercises final authority (Alutto and Belasco, 1972). Based on the range of ways that development organizations use and interpret the term "participation", Pretty (1994) developed a typology of participation as follows:

1. Passive participation, i.e., people are told what to do;

2. Participation in information giving, i.e., people participate by answering questions;

3. Participation by consultation, i.e., people are consulted by external agents but the decision-making power remains with agents;

4. Participation for material incentives, i.e., people participate in return for incentives (i.e., cash or food);

5. Functional participation, i.e., people have a say but only after major decisions have already been made by external agents;

6. Interactive participation, i.e., people participate in joint analysis and take control over local decisions; and,

7. Self-mobilization, i.e., people take control and start action independent of external agents.

These classifications are very much in accord with Narayan's (1995) use of Paul's (1987) four levels of participation. The importance of qualifying the type of participation should be readily apparent. From Pretty's typology, it can be argued that 1 through 5 are phenotypic or pseudo types of participation involving goal-seeking or, at best, multi-goal-seeking behavior. Only Pretty's 6 and 7 (i.e., Interactive Participation and Self-mobilization, respectively) can be considered genotypic or systemic participation involving more than goal-seeking or multi-goal-seeking behavior (e.g., ideal-seeking behavior).

Given the different types of participation, should one expect that all forms of participation will produce the same outcomes? Probably not. To further analyze the structure and function of participation in general, it is useful to compare Pretty's typology of participation with Ackoff and Emery's (1972) "Functional Systems." Based on passive and active structure of actions, and single and multiple function of outcomes, Ackoff and Emery identified seven types of functional systems :

1. Passive Uni-functional system : It can do (passively) only one type of thing in a given environment (e.g., time-telling devices, thermometers).

2. Passive Multi-functional system: It can do (passively) more than one thing in a given environment (e.g., waste emitters).

3. Reactive Uni-functional system: It can (reactively) do only one thing in a given environment (e.g., automatic pilots, thermostats).

4. Reactive Multi-functional system: It can (reactively) do more than one thing in a given environment. It can passively adapt, i.e., discriminate between different environments, but cannot learn (e.g., robots).

5. Active Uni-functional or goal-seeking system: It can (actively) respond (not just react) in more than one way in a given environment in pursuit of just one goal at a time. This system is responsive not reactive, thus, it can "learn" as well as actively adapt (e.g., a tool-utilizing creature such as a bird using a thorn to extract a worm from a hole or a sea utter using a stone to crack an urchin).

6. Active Multi-functional or multi-goal-seeking system: It can (actively) pursue more than one goal at a time in a given environment but cannot determine the goal just the means to pursue it (e.g., computer program). This system can also "learn" and actively adapt.

7. Active Multi-functional or Purposeful system: It can (proactively) pursue more than one goal at a time in a given environment, as well as determine the goal and the means to pursue it, i.e., display reasoned will (e.g., people). It is the only system capable of proactive adaptation (i.e., ideal-seeking behavior).

These seven types of systems are summarized by Ackoff and Emery (Ibid) in a hierarchical order as follows: Ideal-seeking systems Purposeful systems Less-than-goal-seeking systems to multi-goal-seeking systems This hierarchy indicates that all ideal-seeking systems are also purposeful but not all purposeful systems seek ideals (i.e., have the desire and ability to do so). Likewise, all purposeful systems are, by definition, also goal-seeking systems but not all goal-seeking systems can be purposeful (Ibid). A key aspect of Ackoff and Emery's Active Multi-functional or Purposeful Systems, as well as Pretty's Self-Mobilizing Systems, is their ability (i.e., opportunity and resources) to go to the higher end in the hierarchy, that is, to be ideal-seeking. This ability is determined by the directive correlation between system and environment, i.e., the matching of system effectivities (e.g., desire to be ideal-seeking) to the affordances of its environment (e.g., opportunity and resources). In other words, the right environment is crucial for ideal-seeking behavior to be exhibited. Hence, purposefulness, according to Ackoff and Emery (1972), is a producer of ideal-seeking behavior, i.e., a system effectivity. As such, purposefulness is a necessary but insufficient condition for ideal-seeking behavior, just as an acorn alone is a necessary but insufficient condition for an oak tree (Ibid).

Comparing Pretty's typology of participation, Ackoff and Emery's (1972) work on purposeful systems, and the working definition of sustainability used here (i.e., an ecological process characterized by ideal-seeking behavior) it can be argued that, at minimum, Pretty's Interactive Participation, the same as Ackoff and Emery's purposeful behavior, is a necessary (but still insufficient) condition for proactive adaptation or ideal-seeking behavior. Where examples of participation do exist, they are most routinely manifest in terms of goal-seeking or, at best, multigoal-seeking behaviors (where the goal has been determined by somebody else) exemplified by Pretty's participation for material incentives (i.e., "bought" participation) or in Ackoff and Emery's fifth and sixth functional types of systems (i.e., goal-seeking systems). In practice then, individual behavior is still considered instrumental to the organization instead of the organization being instrumental to the individual (i.e., a means towards an end and not as an end in itself) (Carmen, 1990; Narayan, 1995).

This "instrumental" view of individual behavior reinforces the hierarchical approach in organizational (re)designs or re-engineering initiatives and allows for the prevalence of variety-reducing structures (Ackoff and Emery, 1972). Ackoff and Emery (1972) point out that all systems have a constant tendency towards either decreasing or increasing the variety in the range and level of behavior of their component elements. The following quote from their work, On Purposeful Systems, illustrates this: One of the most important characteristics of a system--one that shows why a system is either more or less than the sum of its parts--is the relationship between its behavior (taking the system as an individual) and that of its elements (taking them as individuals). ....(T)he instrumentality of a system tends to be of a lower system order than the system. Thus, although a social system is a purposeful system, all of whose elements are purposeful, there is a constant tendency toward increasing or decreasing variety in the range and level of the behavior of the elements.

In that the individual elements are instrumental to the system, the system will be variety decreasing: the range of purposeful behavior will be restricted, and increasingly behavior will be at a lower level of multi-goal-seeking or goal-seeking behavior. In that the system is instrumental to its component elements, it will tend to be variety increasing: the range of purposeful behavior will be extended, and increasingly behavior will be at the higher level of ideal-seeking (Ackoff and Emery, 1972:215).

Given the increasing interdependencies within our global and turbulent (Type IV) environment, the future of humankind will, in an ever increasing measure, be determined by the choices people make (Emery, 1977). Thus, ideal-seeking behavior must be given serious consideration as the central theme (i.e., necessary and sufficient condition) of any real empowering or organizational (re)design. As Pretty (1994) indicates, long-term economic and environmental revitalization are only possible when people's knowledge is valued and they are given the power to make decisions. In other words, when people are allowed to exhibit the desire for and have the ability to pursue a common ideal. A comparison of the impacts between interactive participation (i.e., Pretty's #6, allowing beneficiaries to take control over local decisions and actions) and consultative participation (i.e., Pretty's #3, simply asking people their opinion) by local people in the implementation of the catchment project in Kenya showed significant differences (Pretty et al., 1995). With the interactive approach, maize yields increased 50 to 200 percent, while with the consultative approach yields increased only 25 percent. Livestock numbers with the interactive approach increased 30 to 50 percent, with the consultative approach only 10 percent. Real wage labor rates increased 100 percent with the interactive approach, whereas with the consultative approach there was no change. With the interactive approach, springs were reappearing and water flows increasing, with the consultative approach neither had occurred (Pretty et al., 1995).

Advocacy of deterministic redesign models of blueprint interventions (e.g., re-engineering, Total Quality Management [TQM], Just In Time [JIT], transfers of technology) or naive, populist processes of participation (e.g., Future Searches, Rapid Rural Appraisals [RRA], Participatory Rural Appraisal [PRA], People's Participation Programmes [PPP]) cannot account for the social, economic, and political forces at play in the interaction of contrasting and conflicting knowledge systems (Thompson and Scoones, 1994).

The need to understand and carefully distinguish among the different types of participation is critical if discussions and expectations of "participation" and goal-seeking vs. ideal-seeking behaviors are to have consistency and validity for understanding their impact on communities and development. For the purposes of this research, "participation" will refer to Pretty's #7, Self-mobilization (i.e., ideal-seeking behavior). In other words, those who must live with the consequences of project outcomes should not only have a say in the decision-making process (from project conception to implementation) and the ability to take control over local decisions, but they should also be able to start action independent of external agents. It is only then, that the instrumental and intrinsic value of participation will come to light (Carmen, 1990). But achieving self-mobilization (i.e., ideal-seeking behavior) is no easy task, particularly when status quo forces prevail supported by rigid organizational structures.

3.4.2 Barriers to Participation

Perhaps the main reason "participation" in general has not occurred on large scale has been the framing of the issue in technological rather than institutional terms (Narayan, 1995). This, Narayan argues, has reduced participation to one more necessary task used or maintained as long as it is convenient or under control (Ibid). All this, he argues, has generated many negative "myths" about participation. These myths include, poor people don't know what is good for them, user decision-making should be limited within well-defined parameters, control should remain with project managers, participatory approaches take a very long time and can only be done on a small scale, when dealing with construction projects, the main indicator of success is construction completed, etc. (Ibid). Many obstacles mitigate against a rapid and pervasive shift from traditional, top-down, expert-based structures to participative and democratic organizational structures. Most of these obstacles are entrenched in social, economic, institutional, and political principles valued in their own right (McCaffrey et al., 1995). Other obstacles are simply "rational," for it seems only "rational" to cling to power by maintaining the status quo (e.g., pushing "development") rather than to voluntarily relinquish power using true empowering and bottom-up approaches. The slow diffusion of truly participative methodologies has also been attributed to their "anti-expert" design which puts consultants and their marketing promotions on the sidelines (Van Eijnatten, 1993). Emery F. (1995) explains the discrepancy between the endorsements and adoption of participative design by tracing the history and evolution of the Socio-Technical System (STS). Although STS was designed to achieve the shift from bureaucratic structures to participative democratic ones, it still relied on a representative process designed by experts and consultants (Emery, 1993). The consultants, who sought to sell it, created an array of techniques and designs that could not and did not deliver what they promised (Grunow, 1995). In addition, STS was an appropriate method for a Type III (disturbed and reactive) environment, not for a Type IV (turbulent) environment. All this complicated further the STS method and its validity giving rise to the fad of re-engineering or "recycled Taylorism" as a last effort to preserve top-down, expert-designed, organizations in a Type IV environment (Emery, F., 1995). Critical knowledge about the needs, uncompensated effects, and priorities of a community (i.e., the effectivities of the system) is held by the community members themselves (Cernea, 1995; Ramón, 1993; Ran, 1985; Salwasser, 1994; Schneider, 1988). Their valuable experience and special understanding of their system and the relationship with its environment cannot be determined from external bureaucratic technospheres (Cernea, 1995; Commoner, 1992; COMUNIDEC, 1993; Ramón, 1995; Salwasser, 1994; UNEP, 1995). Without effective public participation (i.e., at least Interactive Participation) in decision-making processes, and the effective matching of system effectivities and environmental affordances given by the appropriate organizational structure, environmental economics will continue to consist of minor reforms of basic economic models, such as pricing mechanisms, i.e., fiddling with the appearance (phenotype) of an old economic construct, instead of providing for systematic (genotypic) changes in the economic development praxis (Beder, 1996).

3.5 ORGANIZATIONAL DESIGNS

3.5.1 The Bureaucratic or Restrictive First Design Principle (DP1)

Some of the constraints and increasing uncertainties facing development projects are natural (e.g. floods and droughts), while others are man-made (e.g. political infighting and impenetrable bureaucracies). It can be argued that, of these man-made constraints, bureaucracy is the most significant. Information Flows in DP1 Organizations Bureaucracy, as a system for administering organizations involving a specific structure of authority and a clearly defined set of rules and regulations, may be found in large and small, formal or informal, public or private organizations, such as government, corporations, military, churches, schools, political parties, and even households (Boje et al., 1996). Most institutions or organizations can be categorized as having the DP1 organizational design principle exemplified by a dominant hierarchy. In this type of structure, the coordination and control of work is located at least one level above those doing the work (Emery, 1993). Redundancy, essential to the flexibility, adaptability, and viability of all systems (Emery, 1993; Merry, 1997) is incorporated in DP1 structures through dominant hierarchies of redundant "parts." These "parts" constitute the building blocks of DP1 structures (Emery, 1993). The logical properties of DP1 structures are based on what Feibleman and Friend (1945) called "subjective seriality," whereby the governing relation among the parts is that of "asymmetrical dependence," i.e., "the sharing of parts is necessary to one of the parts but not to both" (Ibid:36). This means that errors will "leak" into the system from the environment (Emery, 1977). Because of this asymmetrical dependence, DP1 structures are inherently error-amplifying (Emery, 1977). The governing principle of asymmetric dependence causes the bifurcation of the two primary functions of communication, i.e., to inform and to instruct, thus, reducing communication to a one-way channel, either to inform or to instruct (Emery, 1977). The greater the number of redundant parts, the more opportunity for error and the lower the accuracy of information. DP1 and Environmental Type The bureaucratic or first organizational design principle (DP1) was arguably appropriate for the disturbed and reactive (Type III) environment of a time, i.e., the Industrial Revolution (Emery and Trist, 1973). This type of environment demanded fool-proof and variety reducing organizations by relying solely on top management and the supervisors' ability to ensure a fool-proof organization. This was done by adequately instructing the redundant parts in the levels below what to do and by informing the levels above about the situation under their control. For better accomplishing this, a variety of "carrots and sticks" were (and continue to be) devised. At that time, Weber's regard of bureaucracy as superior to any other form of organization was probably justified. People were (and to some extent still are) considered unreliable and incompetent (hence the need for supervisors). The task, within a DP1 structure, is defined by making the redundant parts as standardized and interchangeable as possible in order to better achieve their function as cogs in a machine (Emery, 1977, 1995).

Learning in a complex and turbulent (Type IV) environment as a DP1 structure Peter Senge (1990) considers five disciplines (i.e., personal mastery, team learning, shared vision, systems thinking and mental models) as essential for a "learning organization." However, organizations do not learn. People do. Learning is a function of the directive correlation between the effectivities of a system and its environmental affordances. Senge's essential disciplines for learning are deliberately restricted or totally lacking in DP1 structures.

Bureaucratic structures keep the people that inhabit them from learning. This is further supported by Weick's (1991:119) analysis of organizations. Perhaps organizations are not built to learn. Instead, they are patterns of means-ends relations deliberately designed to make the same routine response to different stimuli, a pattern which is antithetical to learning.... Organizations are fixed tools in search of new problems, and learning is a relatively minor part of this search. Weick's analysis dealt with DP1 entities. His observations provided support for Geranmayeh's (1992:118) later contention that the structure of the organization has a bearing on those who populate the organization. The issue of organizational barriers to learning is particularly problematic in turbulent and complex environments. Continuous, conscious, conceptual, and experiential learning is a prerequisite for active adaptation and essential for individual and organization survival. In a non-turbulent environment, it was possible to predict, rather accurately, the trajectory of a given system. Hence, it made sense to concentrate most of the resources in the means toward the predicted end (Emery, 1993). Accurate forecasting, however, is very difficult, if not impossible, in an increasingly turbulent and complex environment. In this type of environment people need considerably more freedom to learn and full responsibility for decision-making processes over their own work. Without it, they will not have a knowledgeable, active-adaptive relationship with the environment and they will not be able to behave proactively and as ideal-seeking individuals (Emery, 1995). Participation in a DP1 structure Various forms of involvement often called "participatory" take place in DP1 structures (e.g., Pretty's first four types of participation). But because of the variety-decreasing and error-amplifying nature of these structures, the relationship between the structure and its elements is non-cooperative and dependent. In DP1 structures it is counter to the individual's interest to cooperate with others (e.g. prisoner's dilemma). For people under a DP1 structure, the job environment seems unchanging and there is little, if anything, to be learned. People show apathy, stress, and disaffection (Cabaña, 1995). Under DP1 structures, people may have the desire to behave as cooperative and ideal-seeking individuals, but they do not have the ability (i.e., opportunity and resources) to do so. Not everyone may have the desire to be purposeful, let alone behave as an ideal-seeking individual in pursuit of the satisfaction of human needs. This is logical the result of the maladaptations that have occurred because these individuals have already been subjects of, and have socialized in, a DP1 structure (e.g., adults' inability to view the world from a child's perspective). The physical and psychological pressures inherent in a DP1 structure do not allow for the satisfaction of the psychological requirements for effective work:

1.   Adequate freedom in decision-making

2.   Opportunity for continuous learning

3.   Adequate variety Support and respect

4.   A sense of meaningful work and,

5.   A desirable future (Emery, 1993).

The failure to satisfy these critical human requirements (inherent in the universal ideal of humanity) for effective and purposeful work generates the defense mechanisms and the typical pathologies of bureaucratic structures (Emery, 1994). In DP1 structures, processes and reward systems, such as Management by Objectives (MBO), are not possible (Emery, 1990). The MBO concept was widely acclaimed as a sensible idea when Peter Drucker presented it in 1954. By 1970, the MBO's incompatibility with DP1 structures was realized after having been enthusiastically adopted by major corporations (Levinson, 1970; Kingdon, 1973). As Emery F. (1990:162) puts it, "Attempts to graft MBO onto bureaucracies either failed outright or evolved into a personnel control mechanism for rewarding or punishing managers--a sort of Taylorism for managers." Because in a DP1 structure coordination and control are located as far as possible from the level at which work is being done, objectives cannot be meaningfully formulated. Thus, meaningful objective formulation within a DP1 structure is not possible (Emery, 1990). Similarly, ideal-seeking behavior, manifested through self-mobilization, cooperation, and commitment (the best means for achieving high project performance and addressing negative externalities in the Coasian vein) seem beyond the individual's reach and interest within a DP1 structure. The egocentric nature of DP1 structures leads to an alienated, static and repetitious form of structural organization standing counter to change, knowledge, and novelty (Tulku, 1990). This egocentric nature is not only anti-adaptive but also anti-learning (Bateson, 1972; Weick, 1991). The predictable results of DP1 institutional/organizational factors, which directly and indirectly impose and reinforce negative patterns of thinking and behavior, are: Organizational structure predicated on control, does not foster cooperation and participation. Decision-making and control by supervisors. Workers focus on tasks --the "big picture" is irrelevant/unknown. Narrow and rigidly defined jobs -- complicated work environment. Organizational success ("sustainability") a function of "smart" direction from top.

3.5.2 The Participative Democratic or Enhancing Second Design Principle (DP2)

DP2 systems replace and go beyond Socio Technical Systems (STS). Redundancy, essential to the flexibility, adaptability, and viability of all systems, is incorporated into DP2 systems through redundant functions (Emery, 1993). Humans with redundant functions are the building blocks of DP2 systems (Ibid). DP2 systems are self-managing--but not autonomous --work teams based on a non-dominant hierarchy of functions (see Fig.3-2) as opposed to the dominant hierarchy of "parts" in DP1 structures. Fig. 3-2 The DP2 Organizational Structure Information Flows in DP2 Organizations In DP2 systems, the governing relation between two parts is that of "symmetrical dependence,"i.e., the sharing of parts is necessary to both of the parts (Emery, 1977). Because of this symmetrical dependence, DP2 systems are inherently error-attenuating (Ibid). In a DP2 system the governing principle of symmetric dependence does not cause the bifurcation of the two primary functions of communication, i.e., to inform and to instruct (Emery, 1977), thus assuring effective communication as a two-way channel and attenuating the possibility for error. DP2 and Environmental Type DP2 systems are designed for turbulent (Type IV) environments by those who have to live with the consequences of their actions (or inactions). This design allows for the reconciliation of scientific knowledge (expertise) and ecological knowledge (common sense) based on open-systems theory, ecological learning, and the directive correlation between system and environment. DP2 systems cater to the physical and psychological human aspects and needs (i.e., allow for ideal-seeking behavior) (Emery, 1993). Some of these aspects are an active-adaptive and participative leadership, shared responsibility and accountability, high cooperation and commitment, and effective communication, just the kind of thing missing from most projects (Emery, 1994; Fallon, 1974; Rehm, 1994; Trist and Murray, 1993).

Learning in Complex and Turbulent (Type IV) Environments as a DP2 System In DP2 systems, there is a dynamic balance between the technical structure and the social system designed by those doing the work. In other words, there is continuous learning by the social system., i.e., people at work who are learning consciously, conceptually, experientially, and continuously. Once self-managed groups have a conceptual knowledge of the design principles involved in self management, they can continually evolve their design towards greater group communication, responsibility, commitment (Emery, 1994). This is what gives DP2 organizations the ability to deal with a Type IV environment (i.e., adequately addressing relevant uncertainties, system discontinuities, and negative externalities). DP2 systems may also be viewed from Peter Senge's (1991) perspective as "learning" organizations, i.e., organizations where people continually expand their capacity to create the results they desire, where new and expansive patterns of thinking are nurtured, where collective aspiration is set free, and where people are continually learning how to learn together (Ibid) Participation in a DP2 System Participation in DP2 systems takes the form of either Pretty's Interactive Participation or Self-mobilization (i.e., genotypic participation). In DP2 systems, genotypic participation, cooperation, and commitment are the only viable way to accomplish anything (e.g. mingas). The variety-increasing and error-attenuating nature of DP2 systems allows for a cooperative and mutually dependent relationship between the system and its elements. Under DP2 systems, cooperation is the only way to success for all. DP2 systems allow for the satisfaction of people's psychological requirements for effective work by providing: Adequate freedom in decision-making Opportunity for continuous learning Adequate variety Support and respect A sense of meaningful work, and A desirable future (Emery, 1994). The ability to satisfy these critical human requirements (inherent in the universal ideal of humanity) allows for effective work (Emery, 1993). The DP2 collective consciousness, or system principle, leads to a shared, open, and non-static form of structural organization standing aligned with change and novelty. In other words, the "eco-centric" nature of a DP2 system (as opposed to the "ego"-centric nature of DP1 structure) is actively adaptive (Emery, 1993). Under this type of system, an active-adaptive management process, required for high performance and sustainability, is not only possible but a pre-requisite. In DP2 systems, processes and reward policies, such as Management by Objectives (MBO), are not only possible but necessary (Bragg and Andrews, 1973; Emery, M. 1995, 1996; Fallon, 1974; Trist and Murray, 1993; Van Eijnatten, 1993). The predictable results of DP2 institutional/organizational factors, which enhance and reinforce positive patterns of thinking and behavior, are as follows:

1. Organizational structure predicated on self-management, cooperation and participation

2. Decision-making and control by those doing the work

3. Workers make decisions about tasks--awareness of "big picture" is essential

4. Broad and flexibly defined jobs--uncomplicated work environment

5. Organizational success (sustainability) a function of knowledgeable, and actively adaptive collaborative behavior

The contrasting behavioral implications of bureaucratic and participative democratic organizational structures are summarized in table 3-1.

Table 3-1. Behavioral characteristics of bureaucratic and participative democratic organizational structures (Adapted from Emery, 1993).

MAJOR ASPECTS

BUREAUCRATIC (DP1)	PARTICIPATIVE-DEMOCRATIC (DP2)
Structure state Disrupted, isolated, insecure	Calm, collaborative, secure
Work state Low productivity (high absenteeism, apathy, fatigue, high error rates and accidents)	High productivity (high energy, little absenteeism, low error rates, few accidents). Work Skills Specialized, little cross-functionality Multi-skilled
Psychological Aspects	
Elbow room: Too much or too little (nobody around or boss breathing down the neck)	Optimal
Opportunity to learn: Too much or too little (stress or boredom)	Optimal. Continuous learning and timely feedback Adequate (satisfying work rhythm)
Variety: Too much or too little (stress or boredom)	Optimal. Adequate (self-managed units)
Mutual support and respect: Low (isolated or aligned with	Optimal. Adequate (connected or aligned with

self-serving cliques)	community)
Sense of meaningful work: Too little (little sense of social and personal value of work)	Optimal. Adequate (high sense of social and personal value of work)
Desirable future: Vague, undesirable, or non-existent	Optimal. Clear, self-selected and positive
Emotional tone: Negative, stressful, distrustful	Positive, joyful, trustful
Energy Low, tedious routine	High energy, constant & reasonable challenges
Affect Low, apathetic, disaffectionate	High, energetic, affectionate
Ownership Low or non-existent sense of ownership	High sense of ownership
Commitment Low, nothing to lose	High commitement, plenty to lose
Cooperation Low, counter to individual's interest	High cooperation, only way to accomplish most things
Accountability Low, passing the buck or scape-goating	High, everybody takes responsibility
Participation From Pretty's #1 to #4	Pretty's #6 to #7 (#5 is transitional)
Thinking process Logical (linear), short-range view	Contextualistic (non-linear), long-range view
Modus operandi Based on effectiveness (regardless of the cost)	Based on efficiency (the least cost, sustainably)
Manages change by trying to cope with complexity	Creates change and actively adapts to it
Method depends on organizational policies, procedures, and goals (i.e,Mission)	Method depends on people's ideals, system principle, and values (i.e.,Vision)
Behavior Goal-seeking or multi-goal-seeking	Ideal-seeking and purposeful behavior

Continuity not clear, reactive approach to deal with relevant uncertainties and system discontinuities	Clear, proactive approach to deal with relevant uncertainties and system discontinuities

Given the stark contrast between DP1 and DP2 organizations the choice seems obvious. Yet, the prevalence of DP1 structures contradicts this obvious choice. A logical explanation is that, although most people have a intuitive feeling for the DP2 design (evidenced by "participatory" and "empowerment" efforts), it is not enough to intuit it. Without a conceptual knowledge and understanding of the genotypic design principles involved in organizational design a transformation from a DP1 to a DP2 organization is not possible.

4. MATERIALS AND METHODS

In order to conduct this research, quantitative and qualitative data regarding the selected projects were collected during the months of June, July and August of 1997 through personal interviews with key informants of the projects to be surveyed and analyzed. The informants were selected by means of the Community Reference System (CRS) and were presented with a questionnaire (see Appendix A). The questionnaire was tested by means of psychometric measures for validity and reliability before it was used. Reliability was assessed by means of internal consistency measured by calculating Cronbach's coefficient alpha (Litwin, 1995). The validity of the questionnaire was measured by means of face validity, construct validity, and a pilot project. The survey instrument, which builds upon the Systematic Case Review by Isham et al. (1995), consists of the following:

1. a cover sheet specifying the project background and,

2. a questionnaire composed of 48 questions divided into three sections.

Section I is composed of 20 questions (open-ended and Likert-type) addressing project background (e.g., name, location, budget, implementation dates) and individual statistics (e.g., sex, education, residence). It also provides supporting information about the interviewee's perspective on the project's positive and negative aspects (see Appendix A).

Section II is composed of 12 five-point Likert-type questions (21-32) addressing issues related to project performance (see Appendix A).

Section III is composed of 16 five-point Likert-type questions (33-48) addressing issues related project organizational structure (see Appendix A).

4.1 Research Objectives

In order to test the hypotheses presented in this research, which state that:

The more closely the organizational structure of a project resembles a bureaucracy (DP1), the lower the project performance; and, The more closely the organizational structure of a project resembles a participative democracy (DP2), the higher the project performance, the objectives undertaken were:

A. To determine the performance of the development projects selected in Ecuador based on an index composed of four indicators of project performance; Percentage of project objectives attained;

Percentage of these objectives maintained;

Negative impacts and,

Positive impacts (see Section II of the questionnaire in Appendix A).

B. To identify the organizational structure, or design principle (DP), of the selected projects based on an index composed of seven shadow indicators of organizational structure:

1. Project participation

2. Ownership

3. Accountability

4. Flexibility

5. Communication

6. Cooperation and,

7. Commitment (see Section III of the questionnaire in Appendix A).

C. To conduct a simple linear regression between the dependent variable Project Performance Index (PPI) and the independent variable Organizational Structure Index (OSI), based on the scores obtained for each one, to determine if there is a linear correlation between these two variables ($Y = bX + a$) and, if so, its direction and significance. D. To provide policy recommendations for the conception, design, and implementation of future development projects in Ecuador and throughout the rest of the world.

4.1.1 Methodology for Objective A

This section was designed to address Objective A using 12 Likert-type questions based on four shadow indicators of project performance:

1. Percentage of objectives attained (question 21)

2. Percentage of attained objectives maintained (question 22)

3. Negative project impacts (questions 23-28), and

4. Positive project impacts (questions 29-32). The scores obtained in these 12 questions (21-32) were summed and divided by the number of respondents for each project.

The results obtained were then divided by 12, i.e., the number of questions in this section. The final figures were used to determine the Project Performance Index (PPI) on a scale of 1 to 5. The 12 questions presented in this section were balanced between positive and negative statements and structured in a scale from 1 to 5, so that, the lower the score, the lower the project performance and vice-versa. The closer the mean score of a project approaches the minimum possible value, in the scale of 1 to 5 (i.e., 1), the lower the performance of the project is considered by the respondent. The closer the mean score of a project approaches the maximum possible value (i.e., 5), the higher the performance of the project is considered to be by the respondent.

4.1.2 Methodology for Objective B

This section was designed to address Objective B using 16 Likert-type questions related to organizational structure: 1. Participation in project conception, design, implementation and management (questions 33-38) 2. Ownership of the project (question 39) 3. Project performance accountability (question 40) 4. Project flexibility (questions 41, 42) 5. Communication between project officers and participants (question 43) 6. Cooperation in project design, management and implementation (questions 44-47) 7. Commitment to project success (question 48) The questions in this section were designed to measure whether the projects were bureaucratically structured (i.e., scores <3) or participative democratically structured (i.e., scores >3). The scores obtained in these 16 questions (33-48) were summed and divided by the number of respondents for each project. The results obtained were then divided by 16, i.e., the number of questions in this section. The final figures were used to determine the Organizational Structure Index (OSI) on a scale of 1 to 5. The more closely the mean score of a project approaches the minimum possible value in the scale of 1 to 5 (i.e., 1) the more bureaucratic (DP1) its organizational structure is considered to be. The more closely the mean score of a project approaches the maximum possible value in the scale of 1 to 5 (i.e., 5) the more participative democratic (DP2) its organizational structure is considered to be.

4.1.3 Methodology for Objective C

The Project Performance Index (PPI) and Organizational Structure Index (OSI) of each project were used to conduct a simple linear regression. The task was to specify the regression constants (i.e., b and a) for the regression line ($Y = bX + a$) that best describes the relationship of the two variables based on the least square criterion. The least square criterion states that the best regression line is one which makes the sum of the squared deviations between the points and the regression line a minimum. This was automatically determined by the statistical software SPSS.

4.1.4 Methodology for Objective D

Policy recommendations for the conception, design, and implementation of future development projects were derived from the results of the research.

5. PROJECTS ANALYZED

The projects surveyed and analyzed consisted of 9 development efforts (see Appendix B for project background) implemented along the Ecuadorean Andes, coastal region, and in the Galapagos Islands between 1990 and 1997. They are presented here in the order they were surveyed and analyzed.

1. Environmental Education Program
2. Solid Waste Disposal
3. Tagua Handcrafting
4. Tourist Guide Training
5. Tree Nursery
6. Galapagos Artisanal Fishing/SUBIR
7. Galapagos Agroforestry/SUBIR
8. Cayapas/Cotacachi Reserve/SUBIR
9. Desarrollo Forestal Campesino (DFC)

The choice of these projects was based on financial and time constraints, location accessibility, date of implementation and completion, as well as on fortuitous circumstances. At the outset, only the SUBIR projects were known to be appropriate candidates for survey and analysis. The questionnaire (see Appendix A) was administered in face-to-face interviews to individuals representing a sample ranging from 100 percent to approximately 2 percent of the population involved in each project, totaling 99 individuals for the 9 projects. These individuals interviewed were either community members where the projects were implemented or individuals involved in the projects as paid participants or staff (see Appendix C for details). A mixture of open-ended and fixed questions was used in the survey instrument to obtain the most truthful and complete data from the informants. Open-ended questions are more effective with intimidating circumstances and fixed questions with non-intimidating circumstances (Bernard, 1994; Fink, 1995; Fowler, 1995). A major consideration was the expectation that participant responses would be conditioned by the type of project environment in which the interviewees found themselves (e.g., paid vs. non-paid). The implicit hypothesis being that any form of remuneration builds at least some sense of "loyalty".

6. RESULTS

The addition of projects 1, 2, 3, 4, 5 and 9 proved to be very beneficial to the validity of the analysis adding considerably to the SUBIR projects. The relatively small number of projects surveyed and analyzed, considering the population of projects undertaken in Ecuador during the last decade, by no means diminishes the importance of the results obtained and may be viewed as an opportunity for further research in a more ambitious project.

Section I

Project Background The project budgets ranged from less than $10,000 to more than $500,000. Their location varied from the Andes mountains to the Ecuadorian Coast and the Galapagos Islands. The implementation/completion dates range from 1990 to 1997. The majority of the respondents were non-paid males with primary education. In all cases, only paid employees had an idea of what were the respective project objectives. A modified contingent valuation (CV) method was used to measured the behavioral intention towards paying for the elimination of negative impacts (or accepting compensation for coping with them) and for maintaining benefits derived from the project (or accepting compensation for their lack thereof) as opposed to simply measuring an attitudinal willingness to pay (WTP) (Mitchell and Carson, 1995).

The general feeling of interviewees about projects #1, 2, 3, and 9 was that of satisfaction with the project. The general feeling of interviewees about project #4 was that of moderate satisfaction with the project. The general feeling of interviewees about projects #6, 7, and 8 was that of moderate dissatisfaction with the project. The general feeling of interviewees about project #5 was that of high dissatisfaction with the project. When respondents were asked what they would have changed (if they could have) about the project and why, some of the more interesting responses were the following: Project #1 - Environmental Education "more coordination, cooperation and communication with park officials, is notable the greater interest in projects aimed at increasing economic well-being over environmental education projects." Project #2 - Solid Waste Disposal "more structured organization and greater responsibility, paid jobs, not only based on volunteering." "more participation." "paid jobs." Project #3 - Tagua Handcrafting "some things were changed as requested." "nothing, the training was very good for me. There was nothing else I could do in the community." Project #4 - Tourist Training "hands-on instructions instead of just theory." "would have involved community for better results, so that they may know what the project is all about." Project #5 - Tree Nursery "changing from seedlings for wood for seedlings for ornamentals asking the community first what would they like to do." Project #6 - Galapagos Agroforestry/SUBIR Project supervisor: "I would have changed most of it. Original objectives based on misguided knowledge." A paid employee: "I would have involved the community more to avoid "paternalistic" attitudes and dependency of the people. At the end nothing is left and people get ever more dissatisfied, cynic, and pessimistic about their future." Project #7 - Galapagos Fishery/SUBIR Marine Research Chief Director (who wrote and designed the whole project): "change original objective." "focus on more feasible outcomes." "more participative development." (Note: when asked about whether he considered if his work was appreciated by the community he said: "I have not asked them and I don't care." This statement speaks very eloquently about the directorship of the project.) Chief Communication/education Officer: "would start project from the bottom." "organizational strengthening is the main sustainability problem." "clear objectives and organizational structure." A paid employee: "increase number of project participants, personnel, and economic resources."

The Galápagos fishery project has attracted much internal (Ecuador) and international attention for, in principle, it is focused on directly and indirectly protecting the environmental and hence, economic, integrity of the world's most treasured resources. Interviews with the directors of two of the fisheries cooperatives were of particular interest and are summarized as follows: "We never really participated in the so called 'project', from our perspective there has not been such a thing. The management plan was never implemented. We would have liked to have seen training workshops on fishing and some of the monies collected from tourists (up to $80/person) used in our benefit, but most of it goes to the central government in the capital and the little left here is squandered by the municipality. But the bulk of the benefits derived from the Islands (from tourism and fishing) goes to major tourist operators (tourist packages are pre-arranged inland by big tourist operators) and large scale fishing companies who deplete our marine resources with the knowledge and consent of the authorities. We are constantly being told "not to do this", "not to do that", and no alternatives are offered. What the artisanal fishing sector needs is: constant capacitation in cooperative building, conservation, human relations and natural resource management. a law (implemented and enforced) to protect the resources around the islands for exclusive use of small fishing cooperatives legally incorporated in Galapagos, declaring the zone as protected from industrial activities (the real threats to the islands). In addition, declaring 40 nautic miles around the islands as conservation area for sustainable use. a project aimed at mariculture of the species of greater demand such as lobster, sea cucumber, sea shells, etc. so that fishermen may get a real sense of the need to protect the resources and at the same time may be allowed to perceived an income from their work in order not just to survived but to improve their living conditions. that the government provide financing for management of the islands (i.e., control of real predators, such as, big ships), creation of laboratories for scientific investigation and a sustainable fishing schedule for all the resources in the long-term. We are park rangers with no pay and mistreated by pseudo-ecologists who when an opportunity appears fill their pockets with dollars in the name of the Galapagos." Project #8 - Cayapas Cotacachi Reserve/SUBIR The Cayapas Cotacachi Reserve is a very important component of the SUBIR project. The importance of this component is not only based on the richness of the biological resources of the reserve but only on the livelihoods of many communities living along the Cayapas river and its tributaries. The more interesting responses from interviewees were: From a coordinator of one of the SUBIR components: - "I would have changed the organization of the community if I had the knowledge and tools to do so, for this is the main weakness of the project" From a project technician: "boost work in the field." From community members: "allow for real empowerment of the people." "more diverse production, especially for meat products (pigs, beef, fish) and products more suitable for the region (e.g., pineapples, bananas) instead of the ones offered (e.g.,corn)." "organizing community." "proving paid work for the people (not hiring from outside)." "more training." A majority (>70%) of respondents of project #8 answered that they did not know what they would have changed if they had had the opportunity to do so. Project #9 - Desarrollo Forestal Campesino (DFC) "more incentives (e.g. higher pay) to field workers and extensionists so that they may be more committed to their work." "other means of production in the short-term." "more economic resources for salaries, marketing and investigation."

Section II

Project Performance The minimum possible score for project performance (i.e., questions 21-32) was 12, that is, if all the 12 questions had been given a 1. The maximum possible score was 60, that is, if all the 12 questions had been given a 5. The mean scores obtained for the performance of each project are shown in Table 6-1.

Table 6-1. Project Performance Scores for Each Project.
Project # Project Name: Score
1 Environmental Education Program 39

2 Solid Waste Disposal 45.62

3 Tagua Handcrafting 41.67

4 Tourist Guide Training 34.33

5 Tree Nursery 22.81 (table continues)

6 Galapagos Artisanal Fishing/SUBIR 27.33

7 Galapagos Agroforestry/SUBIR 34.2

8 Cayapas/Cotacachi Reserve/SUBIR 33

9 Desarrollo Forestal Campesino (DFC) 46.33

Highest: 46.33 Lowest: 22.81 Mean: 36.03

Section III

Project Organizational Structure The scores obtained for each project were summed and divided by the number of respondents for each project. The minimum possible score for project organizational structure (questions 33-48) was 16, i.e., if all the 16 questions had been marked 1. The maximum possible score was 80, i.e., if all the 16 questions had been marked 5. Table 6-2 shows the mean scores obtained for the organizational structure of each project. Table 6-2. Organizational Structure Scores for Each Project.

Project # Project Name: Score

1 Environmental Education Program 52

2 Solid Waste Disposal 58.62

3 Tagua Handcrafting 55

4 Tourist Guide Training 42.33

5 Tree Nursery 18.56

6 Galapagos Artisanal Fishing/SUBIR 32.33

7 Galapagos Agroforestry/SUBIR 35.2

8 Cayapas/Cotacachi Reserve/SUBIR 25

9 Desarrollo Forestal Campesino (DFC) 44.78

Highest: 58.62 Lowest: 18.56 Mean: 40.42

Performance and Organizational Structure Indexes The scores obtained in Section II were divided by 12 (i.e., the number of questions in this section) and used to determine the Project Performance Index (PPI) for each project (see Table 6-3). The scores obtained in Section III were divided by 16 (i.e., the number of questions in this section) and used to determine the Organizational Structure Index (OSI) for each project (see Table 6-3). Table 6-3 indicates the scores for the Project Performance Index (PPI) and Organizational Structure Index (OSI) obtained for each project on a scale of 1 to 5. Table 6-3 Project Performance Index (PPI) and Organizational Structure Index (OSI) Project # Project Name: PPI OSI

Project #	Project Name	PPI	OSI
1	Environmental Education Program	3.25	3.25
2	Solid Waste Disposal	3.80	3.66
3	Tagua Handcrafting	3.47	3.44
4	Tourist Guide Training	2.86	2.65
5	Tree Nursery	1.90	1.16
6	Galapagos Artisanal Fishing/SUBIR	2.27	2.02
7	Galapagos Agroforestry/SUBIR	2.85	2.20
8	Cayapas/Cotachachi Reserve/SUBIR	2.75	1.56
9	FAO/DFC	3.86	2.80

Highest: 3.86 3.66 Lowest: 1.90 1.16 Mean: 3.00 2.53

It should be noted that projects 9, 7, 8, and 6 had a higher ratio of paid vs. non-paid participants than the other projects. Paid participants may feel greater responsibility toward project outcomes than non-paid participants, and, thus, paid participants may see greater positive outcomes . This provides one plausible explanation for the relatively high PPI scores of these projects. The simple linear regression, conducted with the statistical software SPSS using the PPI and OSI values, produced the following results: R Square = .7341 F = 19.3252 Significant F = .0032 From Table 6-3 a correlation between project performance and organizational structure is evident. This correlation is supported by the results from the simple linear regression conducted . The results indicate a strong correlation ($r2 = 0.73$) between the dependent variable Project Performance Index (PPI) and the independent variable Organizational Structure Index

(OSI). The regression equation, $Y = 0.661X + 1.3309$, indicates a slope of the regression line of 0.661 (p = 0.0032) and a value for the constant a of 1.3309. This is a fundamental finding of this research. It indicates that the more the organizational structure of a project resembles DP2, i.e., the higher the OSI scores, the higher the project performance, i.e., the higher the PPI scores. The hypotheses that projects with an organizational structure that more closely resembles a bureaucracy (low OSI scores) reduce project performance and increase negative impacts (low PPI scores), and projects with an organizational structure that more closely resembles a participative-democratic organizational structure (high OSI scores) enhance project performance in general, and reduce negative impacts in particular (high PPI scores), are strongly supported ($r2 = 0.73$).

7. DISCUSSION OF RESULTS

The results of this research strongly support the general conclusion that the behaviors exhibited by project participants in the nine Ecuadorian projects analyzed here was the predictable result of the organizational structure within which these behaviors took place. The type of participation exhibited in these projects ranged from Pretty's Passive Participation (e.g., project #1,3,4, 5, 6, 7, 8, 9), to, at best, Pretty's Active Participation (e.g., project #2). Concomitantly, the behavior exhibited by the project participants ranged from individualistic goal-seeking, i.e., $OSI < 3$, (e.g., projects #4, 5, 6, 7, 8, 9) to cooperative multi-goalseeking, i.e., $OSI > 3$ but < 5 (e.g., project#1, 2, 3). The most striking results are those of Project #2, the one with the highest summed PPI and OSI scores, and Project #5, the one with the lowest scores. These two projects were conducted with very similar communities (i.e., ~30 families) within the Machalilla National Park (MNP), and both were sponsored by the same NGO. The only difference was the design and implementation of these two projects. Project #2 was basically conceived and implemented by the community members themselves, with the support of a national NGO. Project #5 was conceived by the national NGO and superimposed on the community. When the benefits, characteristic of projects with higher PPI and OSI (i.e., projects #1, 2, 3) are revisited, it is evident that they are closely aligned with the expectations for a participative-democratic DP2 organization and ideal-seeking behavior that is possible within such organizational structure. However, it must be understood that this does not imply that the projects that display positive behaviors, such as high participation and commitment, and positive outcomes (e.g., Project #2) are necessarily formally organized to achieve these behaviors and positive outcomes. The reality for the projects examined is that, they are not.

In real-world situations, positive behaviors (i.e., high OSI scores), such as those exhibited by participants of project #2, and positive outcomes (i.e., high PPI scores), are more likely associated with the values and behaviors of specific project managers and organizational leaders than on expert knowledge of participative-democratic design principles (DP2-). While such situations are locally positive, they are not systemic. Positive characteristics, or DP2-like environments (that are supervisor-personality dependent), can change overnight with a change in leadership (go from DP2- to DP1-). Clearly, it is not enough that those who must live with the consequences of project outcomes conceive, design and implement projects. For sustainability, they must also be provided with the conceptual understanding of the design principles involved in a participative-democratically designed project. That is, it is not enough to be purposeful and have the desire to progress toward an ideal. If this desire is to have any meaning, it must be accompanied by the ability (i.e., opportunity and resources, such as decision-making capability, freedom to act, and knowledge about organizational design principles) to progress towards the desired ideals. This cannot be emphasized too much. Virtually all development initiatives, regardless of initial financial conditions, eventually become the "property" of those who must continue to live with them. Where project perceptions, participation and loyalty are primarily a function of compensation and/or personalities, the prospects for sustainability are practically non-existent. In terms of sustainability, projects #5, 6, 7, and 8, have already been abandoned by the community (or it is just a matter of time before their failure is acknowledged). The sustainability of projects #1, 2, 3, 4 and 9 is also in doubt. Although these projects may have an organizational structure that more closely resembles a participative democracy than a bureaucracy, there is not a clear and conceptual understanding, on the part of the participants (project officers and community members), of the design principles involved. Hence, their organization is vulnerable to pressure to "get organized", i.e., to be more DP1, the familiar, although critically dysfunctional, model. Particularly, where continued volunteer participation is a key element in sustainability.

8. CONCLUSIONS AND RECOMMENDATIONS

The results from this research provide both a theoretical framework for understanding, and an empirical test of the hypotheses suggested by the literature on project outcomes. More specifically, the results illustrate the relationship of project outcomes to project organizational structure. The relationship of project performance (i.e., high PPI scores) with project structures that incorporate a particular type of participation (i.e., high OSI scores) in design and implementation has been shown in the literature review and by the empirical evidence presented here to be significantly correlated. The relationship of project effectiveness with project structures that incorporate more than just goal-seeking types of beneficiary participation has also been shown here to be strongly correlated The formal organizational structure (i.e., bureaucratic vs. participative-democratic) within which nominal beneficiary participation (i.e., goal-seeking vs. ideal-seeking behavior) takes place is crucial. Bureaucratic organizational structures have not delivered satisfactory outcomes in the context of development initiatives. Most often, it seems likely that no alternative organizational design was even considered by project officials. Even where projects were rigidly structured to produce a "fool-proof" system, failure was probably inevitable. It is often remarked that (even in pay-for-work situations) this is "because the fools are too clever!" Where participants are volunteers, the best case scenario is that they walk away. The worst case scenario may even involve sabotaging. Bureaucracies, by design, restrict the behavior of their elements by using a range of strategies (e.g., from coercion to goal-seeking incentives). This is a far cry from allowing individuals to manifest ideal-seeking behavior. The difference between a goal-seeking (or multi-goal-seeking) individual, and an ideal-seeking one, is particularly important in a turbulent environment characterized by increasing relevant uncertainties and system discontinuities. A turbulent environment demands continual active adaptation, and goals/objectives need to be constantly redefined based on time-free and intrinsically adaptive guidelines. Only ideals meet these criteria (Emery, 1993).

The isolated, mechanistic, and competitive DP1 structure, characterized by its variety-decreasing (restrictive range of choice, i.e., "fool-proof") and error-amplifying nature, has been shown here to be strongly correlated with poor project performance and unsustainable outcomes. This is the predictable result of institutional/organizational factors which, directly and indirectly, impose and reinforce negative patterns of thinking and behavior. Within this organizational structure, participation ranges from Pretty's #1, or Passive Participation, to, at best, Pretty's #4, or "Bought" Participation (i.e., goal-seeking behavior). When this organizational structure is replaced by a collaborative and participative democratic system, negative patterns of thinking and behavior change, leading to sustainable outcomes and to the reduction/elimination of negative externalities. Only the variety-increasing, error-attenuating nature of participative democratic DP2 systems allows for higher types of participation, ranging from Pretty's #6, or Interactive Participation, to Pretty's #7 Self-mobilization, i.e., for ideal-seeking behavior.

The future of our global environment requires that governments, such as that of Ecuador, and aid organizations, such as The World Bank, IMF, USAID, and local and international NGOs, reconsider the criteria for project design and implementation before attempting to implement any project and waste even one additional sucre! It is at the outset that social, institutional, environmental, and economic variables involved in every project must be adequately addressed. Those who must live with the consequences of project outcomes must, systematically, have the ownership and the decision-making capabilities from project design and implementation to the sustainable maintenance of the desired outcomes. The need for organizational restructuring for compliance with ISO 9000 and ISO 14000 and survival in a turbulent and complex environment is acknowledged and accepted throughout the world. What is still disputed, particularly by those who favor the status quo (i.e., those who stand to lose if power relations change), is the type of organizational (re)structuring as well as the means to achieve it. Most advocates of organizational restructuring (e.g., traditional Organization Theory consultants) are fixated with phenotypic or pseudo changes of organizational structure, purposefully or inadvertently ignoring genotypic changes. The critical need for genotypic organizational restructuring (through conscious, conceptual, and experiential knowledge of organizational design principles) for active adaptation and survival in a complex and turbulent environment seems to escape even the most avant-garde chaos theorists and consultants (e.g., Fitzgerald, 1997). The benefits of increased commitment and participation, while viewed as positive and desirable, have not been definitively attributed by most conventional organizational theorists and consultants to genotypic organizational design, but to more "efficient" bureaucratic (re)designs. These "efficient" (re)designs, simply stress the need for "participatory" decision-making processes, while attempting, unsuccessfully, to maintain their characteristically bureaucratic dominant hierarchy under disguise. Policy making in general, and on environmental issues in particular, must be made in the context of uncertainty. Although no particular land-use practice can be said to be sustainable, by building in institutional flexibility, through a formal participative democratic system, organizations can better cope with uncertainty and thereby avoid unsustainable practices and negative externalities going beyond compliance with ISO 9000 and ISO 14000.

USAID (1996) was correct when stating that unless men, women, and children change their behavior with regards to the use of natural and man-made resources there is little, if any, hope for sustainable development. But, as was argued in Chapter 2 of this research, human behavior (i.e., system effectivity) is only half of the equation in the model of directive correlation between system and environment. The other half (i.e., environmental affordances) is given by the organizational structure within which human behavior takes place. It may not always be possible to create ideal-seeking systems. It is possible, however, to create the necessary and sufficient conditions for their emergence by use of the correct organizational design principle (i.e., DP2) for systems to be purposeful and, in appropriate circumstances, exhibit ideal-seeking behavior. A modified Coasian approach (i.e., a cooperative-bargaining process), as discussed in chapter 2, could only be productively undertaken within a DP2 organizational design, where timely feedback is possible, transaction costs are low, and where it is in the individual interest to cooperate (Emery, 1993, 1995).

The "function" of economics has always been to allocate scarce means, most efficiently, among given ends. But the ends cannot be defined by economic theory alone, nor by the natural sciences. This highlights the need for ethics, morals, and universal ideals as the foundation upon which economics and the natural sciences must rest. Weighing costs and benefits is an inherent part of human reasoning and purposefulness. When people perceive the potential benefits of an action as greater than the perceived costs, then the action will take place and vice-versa. People within projects based on the second design principle (DP2) will be able to exhibit ideal-seeking behavior and perceive greater benefits than if they were in an organizational structure that more closely resembles DP1. Effectively increasing project performance, i.e., not only attaining project objectives and maintaining the desired outcomes, but also reducing or eliminating negative impacts and externalities. An increased understanding of the role played by the organizational structure, or design principles, of development projects in the sustainability of the desired outcomes, and in the reduction/elimination of negative externalities, will contribute to identifying the paradigm shift needed to achieve the desired redirection towards a path of social stability and well-being, environmental friendliness, and sustainable economic development in Ecuador and

elsewhere. To adequately deal with the relevant
uncertainties of our times, it is crucial to have in place
DP2 systems which optimize the potential responsiveness
of the system to change through a continuous, conscious,
active-adaptive relationship with the environment
(Emery, 1985; Katz & Kahn, 1966). Only DP2 systems
allow for the optimal matching of systems' effectivities to
environmental affordances, i.e., to be proactively
adaptive.
Agenda 21 from the 1992 Rio Summit spurred the re-
emergence of the perceived need for an alternative
development approach for the management of our
environments (i.e., natural, social, institutional, and
economic). This development approach must be pursued,
at the local-to-global level and through Open Systems
Theory based planning (e.g., Search Conferences and
Participative Design Workshops) and participative
democratic organizations. The peoples themselves must
"own" the processes and the consequences, not external
institutions or organizations, for it is the local people who
must live with project outcomes (good and/or bad).

REFERENCES

Abrahamsson, B. (1993). Why organizations? Sage
Publications Inc.
Ackoff, R.L & Emery, F.E. (1972). On purposeful
systems. Aldine-Atherton, New York.
Allen, W.J., Bosh, O.J. & Gibson, R.G. (1996). Farmers
and scientists working together to achieve more
sustainable land management. On line,
http://www.landcre.cri.nz/kip/afres.htm
Alutto, J. A., & Belasco, J. A. (1972). A typology for

participation in organizational decision making.
Administrative Science Quarterly, 17(1), 117-125.

Anderson, V. (1991). Alternative Economic Indicators.
NY: Routledge.

Ameyaw, S. (1992). Sustainable development and the
community: Lessons from the KASHA Project.
Environmentalist, 12 (4).

Angyal, A. (1941). Foundations for science of
personality. Harvard University Press.

Antonovsky, H. (1993). Complexity, conflict chaos,
coherence, coercion and civility. Social Science and
Medicine, 37(8), 969-974.

Argyris, C. (1955). Organizational leadership and
participative management. Journal of Business 28 (55), 1-
7. _____ (1958). The organization: What makes it
healthy? Harvard Business Review, March-April 1958,
107-116. _____ (1982). The executive mind and
double-loop learning. Organizational Dynamics, Autumn
1982, 5-22.

Argyris, C. & Schon, D. A. (1978). Organizational
Learning: A theory of action perspective. Reading. MA:
Addison-Wesley.

Asch, S.E. (1952). Social Psychology. Prentice-Hall.

Ashby, W.R. (1952). Design for a brain. London:
Chapman & Hall.

Atkins, M.H. & Lowe, J.F. (1977). Pollution control costs
in industry. Pergamon Press.

Banham, R. (1995-April). A changing world: science,
business and risk prediction. Risk Management, 21-31.

Barzelay, M. (1992) Breaking through bureaucracy.
Berkeley, CA: University of California Press Ltd. Bates,
R.H. (1991). Anthropology and development: A note on
the structure of the field. In Putting People First.
Sociological Variables in Rural Development. Oxford
University Press.

Bateson, G. (1972). Steps to an ecology of mind. Mew
Yok: Ballantine.

Bathrick, D. (1997) Fostering sustainable global well-being: A new paradigm to revitalize agriculture and rural development. On line:
http://www.worldbank.org/html/fpd/technet/bathrick.htm
Beckerman, W. (1992). Economic Growth and the Environment: Whose Growth? Whose Environment? World Development, 20 (4), 481-496.
Beder, S. (1996). The environment goes to market. [Online]. http://www.uow.edu.au/
Bennett, J. (1988). Anthropology and development: The Ambiguous engagement. In Production and Autonomy: Anthropological Studies and Critiques of Development, Monographs in Economic Anthropology, 5, John Bennett and John Bowens (Eds.) University Press of America.
Bentley, J.W. (1994). Facts, fantasies and failures of participatory research. Agriculture and Human Values. 11 (2&3), 140-150.
Bernard, H. (1994). Research methods in anthropology: qualitative and quantitative approaches. Sage publications Inc. USA. Berry, W.D. (1984). Nonrecursive causal models. Quantitative Applications in the Social Sciences. Series 07-037. SAGE Publications Inc. Bertlin, J (1994). Assessing the economic and environmental impact of UK overseas aid for water development projects: Sustainability lessons from the NAO review process. Kent, UK: Wye College. Project Appraisal, 9 (4), 263.
Beveridge, W.I.B. (1950). The art of scientific investigation. NY: Vintage Books.
Bion, W.R. (1961). Experiences in Groups. NY: Basic Books Inc.
_____ (1952). Group dynamics: A review. International Journal of Psychoanalysis. 33, 235-247.
Boje, D.M. (1997). The neglect of Fred Emery's theories in organization theory texts. Unpublished paper (October 27, 1997). Boje, D.M., Gephart, R.P., & Thatchenkery, T.J. (Eds.) (1996). Postmodern management and organization theory. Sage Publications Inc. Bos, L.

(1994). Environment and disease: Ever growing concern. Environmental Conservation, 21 (2), 98-103.

Boyer, W.W. (1964). Bureaucracy on Trial. New York: The Bobbs-Merrill Company Inc.

Bragg, J.E., & Andrews, I.R. (1973). Participative decision-making: An experimental study in a hospital. The Journal of Applied Behavioral Science, 9(6), 727-735.

Brandenburg, A.M., Carrol, M.S., & Blatner, K.A. (1995). Towards successful forest planning through locally based qualitative sociology. Western Journal of Applied Forestry, 10 (3), 95-100.

Bromley, D.W. (1995). Handbook of environmental economics. Basil Blackwell Ltd., Cambridge, Massachusetts.

Brown, L.R., Kane, H. & Ayres, E. (1993). The Trends that are shaping our Future: Vital Signs. World Watch Institute.

Buchholz, S. & Roth T. (1987). Creating the high performance team. New York:Wiley.

Burns, T. & Stalker, G.M. (1961). The management of innovation. Tavistock Publications. Burnside, D.G. & Chamala, S. (1994). Ground-based monitoring: A process of learning by doing. Rangel J.. 16 (2), 221-237.

Cabaña, S. (1994). Participative design works, partially doesn't. In The Journal for Quality and Participation. 18 (1), 10-19. Cadwell, L.K. (1990). Between two worlds. Cambridge University Press. 38-84;105- 123.

Carley, M.,& Christie, I. (1993). Managing sustainable development. Minneapolis, MN: University of Minnesota Press.. Carmen, R. (1990). Communication, education and empowerment. Manchester Monographs: University of Manchester.

Carnevale, D.G. (1995). Trustworthy government. Leadership and management strategies for building trust and high performance. San Francisco: Jossey- Bass Publishers. CDIE (1990). AID evaluations news. Focus

on sustainability. Thompson R. J. (Ed.) Washington, DC.
Cernea, M. (1991). Knowledge from social science for
development policies and projects. In Putting People
First. Sociological Variables in Rural Development.
Oxford University Press.

_____ (1995). Social Organization and Development
Anthropology. Malinowsky award lecture. Human
Organization. Society for Applied Anthropology, 54 (3).
Chein, I. (1972). The science of behavior and the image
of man. NY: Basic Books. Churchman, C.W. (1968).
Challenge to reason. NY: McGraw-Hill Book Company.

_____ (1971). The design of inquiring
systems: basic concepts of systems and organization. NY:
Basic Books.

_____ (1979). The systems approach and its
enemies. NY: Basic Books, Inc.

_____ (1982). Thought and wisdom.
California: Intersystems Publications.

_____, Auebach, L., & Sadan, S. (1975).
Thinking for decisions. Deductive quantitative methods.
Science Research Associates, Inc.

Coase, R. (1960). The problem of social cost. Journal of
Law and Economics, 3 (1), 1-44. Cocks, K.D. & Walker,
B.H. (1994). Contribution of 'sustainability' criteria to
social perceptions of land use options. Land Degradation
and Rehabilitation, 5, 143- 151. NY: John Wiley & Sons.
Cohn, J.P. (1989). Iguana conservation and economic
development. Bioscience, 39, 359-63. Common, M.
(1995). Sustainability and policy. Cambridge, UK:
Cambridge University Press. Commoner, B. (1992).
Making peace with the planet. New York: New Press.
COMUNIDEC (1993). Manual de planeamiento andino
comunitario: El PAC en la region andina. Sistema de
Investigacion y Desarrollo Comunitario and the World
Resources Institute. Quito-Ecuador Connor, J.D., Perry,
G.M., & Adams, R.M. (1995). Cost-effective abatement
of multiple production externalities. Water Resources

Research, 31 (7), 1789- 1796.

Collins, D. (1995). A socio-political theory of workplace democracy: Class conflict, constituent reactions and organizational outcomes at a gainsharing facility. Organization Science. 6 (6), 628-643.

Cordato, R.E. (1992). Welfare economics and externalities in an open ended universe: A modern Austrian perspective. London: Kluwer Academy Publishers.

Costanza, R., Ed. (1990). Ecological economics: The science and management of sustainability. New York: Columbia University Press.

Cropper, M.L., & Oates, W.E. (1992). Environmental economics: a survey. Journal of Economic Literature, 30, 675-740. Cumming, T.G. & Srivastva, S. (1977). Management of work: a socio-technical systems approach. CA: San Diego. University Associates.

Dachler, H.P., & Wilpert, B. (1978). Conceptual dimensions and boundaries of participation in organizations: A critical evaluation. Administrative Science Quarterly, 23, 1-39.

De Janvry A., Sadoulet, E., & Santos, B. (1994). Project appraisal for sustainable rural development: Some note for IFAD. International Bank for Reconstruction and Development. Staff working Paper 17.

Daly, H.E. (1968). On economics as a life science. Journal of Politics and Economics, 76, 392-406.

_____(1991). Speculations.Towards an environmental macroeconomics. Land Economics, May 1991, 67 (2), 255-59.

_____ & Townsend K.N. (Eds.). (1993). Valuing the Earth: Economics, Ecology, Ethics. Cambridge: The MIT Press. Damasio, R.A. (1994). Descartes' error: Emotion, reason, and the human brain. NY: Putnam's Books.

DeVellis, R.F. (1991). Scale development. Applied Social Research Methods. Series 26. London:SAGE Publications Ltd. Diario Hoy (1995, November 5).

Boletin de Noticias Ecuanet [Online}. Available e-mail:
Hoy@edimpres.com.ec.. Diemer, J., & Alvarez, R.
(1995). Sustainable Community, Sustainable Forestry.
Journal of Forestry, 93 (11), 10-14. Dietz, F.J. & Van der
Straten, J. (1992). Rethinking environmental economics:
Missing links between economic theory and
environmental policy. Journal of Economic Issues, 26 (1),
27-51.

Dlot, J.W., Altieri, M.A. & Masumoto, M. (1994).
Exploring the theory and practice of participatory
research in US sustainable agriculture: A case study in
insect pest management. Agriculture and Human Values,
11 (2 & 3), 126-139. Douthwaite, R. (1993). The Growth
Illusion. Tulsa: Council Oaks books.

Downs, A. (1967). Inside Bureaucracy. Boston:Little
Brown. Drucker, P.F. (1954). The practice of
management. Harper, New York. Duchin, F. & Lange, G.
(1994). The Future of the Environment. New York:
Oxford University Press. Dunn-Rankin, P. (1983).
Scaling Methods. New Jersey: Lawrence Erlbaum
Associates, Publishers.

Durkheim, E. (1997). The division of labor in society.
NY: The Free Press.

Emery, M.(1997). Open systems is alive and well. Paper
presented before the Academy of Management meetings,
ODC revision session "Rethinking Sociotecnical System
Theory."

_____ (Ed.) (1993). Participative Design for
Participative Democracy. Canberra: The Australian
National University. Centre for Continuing Education.

_____ (1994). The Search Conference: State of the
Art 1994. Canberra: The Australian National University.
Centre for Continuing Education.

_____ (1995). Searching. Amsterdam & Philadelphia:
John Benjamin Publishing..

_____ & Purser R. (1996). Search Conferences in
Action. CA: Jossey-Bass.

Emery, F.E. (1993). Policy: Appearance and reality, Chapter 6 in, A Systems-based approach to policymaking, Kenyon B.DeGreene (Ed.), Boston: Kluwer Academic Publishers.

_____ (1995). Participative design: effective, flexible and successful, now! The Journal for Quality and Participation, 18 (1), 6-9.

_____ (1990). Management by objectives. In participative design for participative democracy. Merrelyn Emery (Ed.) (1993). Canberra: The Australian National University. Centre for Continuing Education.

_____ (1985). Matching effectivities to affordances in design jobs. In Participative Design for Participative Democracy. Merrelyn Emery (Ed.). Canberra: The Australian National University. Centre for Continuing Education. _____ (Ed.) (1981). Systems thinking. Penguin Books Inc. Victoria, Australia.

_____ (1977) Futures we are in. Leiden: Martinus Nijhoff Social Science Division.

_____ (1976). Causal path analysis. In Fred Emery (Ed.) (1981). Systems thinking. Penguin. 1(1), 293-298.

_____ & Thorsrud, E. (1969). Form and content in industrial democracy. Tavistock, London.

_____ & Trist E.L. (1973). Towards a social ecology. NY: Plenum Press.

_____ & _____ (1965). The causal texture of organizational environments. Human Relations, 18, 21-32. _____ & Oeser, O.A. (1958). Information, decision, and action. Australia: Melbourne University Press.

Esman, M.J. & Uphoff, N.T. (1984). Local organizations: Intermediaries in rural development. London: Cornell University Press.

Fallon, K.P., Jr. (1974). Participatory management: An alternative in human service delivery systems. Child Welfare, 53, 555-562.

Feibleman, J. & Friend, J.W. (1945). The structure and

function of organization. Philosophical Review, 54, 19-44. Fink, A. (1995). The survey handbook. CA: Sage Publications Inc. Thousand Oaks.

_____ (1995). How to design surveys. CA: Sage Publications Inc. Thousand Oaks.

_____ (1995). How to ask survey questions. CA: Sage Publications Inc. Thousand Oaks.

Finsterbush, K. & Van Wicklin III, W. (1987). The contribution of beneficiary participation to development project effectiveness. Public Administration and Development, 7, 1-23. Fizdale, R. (1974). The voluntary agency: Structure vs. accountability. Social Casework, 55, 478-483.

Fitzgerald, L. (1997). Living on the Edge. On line:www.orgmind.com /chaos.

Folmer, H. & van Ierland, E. (Eds.) (1989). Valuation methods and policy making in environmental economics. Amsterdam : Elsevier.

Fordham, G. (1993). Sustaining local involvement. Community Development Journal, 28 (4), 299-304.

Fowler, F.J.Jr. (1995). Improving survey questions. Design and evaluation. CA: Sage Publications Inc.Thousand Oaks. Fritz, R. (1989). The Path of Least Resistance. NY: Fawcett Book Group.

Funtowicz, S.O., & Ravetz, J.R. (1991). A new scientific methodology for global environmental issues. In Robert Costanza (Ed.) Ecological Economics: The science and management of sustainability. New York: Columbia University Press. Geranmayeh, A. (1992). Organizational learning through interactive planning: Design of learning systems for ideal-seeking organizations. University of Pennsylvania. Ph.D. Dissertation.

Giampietro, M. & Bukkens, S. (1992). Sustainable development: Scientific and ethical assessments. Journal of Agricultural and Environmental Ethics, 28-57.

Gibson, J.J. (1983). The senses considered as perceptual systems. Illinois: Waveland Press Inc. Prospects Heights.

Goodykoontz, L.,& Miller, M.H. (1990). Does participatory management make a difference? Journal of Nursing Administration, 20 (6), 7-29.

Gordon, T.J. (1992) Chaos in social systems. Technological forecasting and social change, 42 (1), 1-16.

Gormley, W.T. Jr. (1989). Taming the Bureaucracy. Princeton, N.J.: Princeton University Press.

Gregersen, H., & Sailer, L. (1993) Chaos theory and its implications for social science research. Human Relations, 46 (7), 777-802. Grunow, D. (1995). The research design in organization studies: Problems and prospects. Organization Science, 6 (1), 93-103.

Hart, S.L. (1992). An integrative framework for strategy-making processes. Academy of Management Review, 17, 334. Hartup, B.K. (1994). Community conservation in Belize: Demography, resource use, and attitudes of participating landowners. Biological Conservation, 69, 235- 241.

Heider, F. (1958). The Psychology of interpersonal relations. NY:John Wiley & Sons Inc. Hirst, P. (1994). Associative Democracy. Amberts: The University of Massachusetts Press.

Hirsch, S.H. & Shulman, L.C. (1976). Participatory governance: A model for shared decision-making. Social Work in Health Care, 1 (4), 433-446.

Homer-Dixon. T.F., Boutwell, J.H. & Rathjens, G.W. (1993). Environmental change and violent conflict. Scientific American, February, 1993, 38-45.

Howarth, R.B. (1996) Status effects and environmental externalities. Ecological Economics, 16 (1), 25-34.

Hudson, N. (1991). A study of the reasons for success or failure of soil conservation projects. FAO soils bulletin 64. Rome: Food and Agriculture Organization.

Hyneman, C.S. (1950) Bureaucracy in a democracy. New York: Harper and Brothers Publishers. IFAD (1995). Conference on hunger and poverty. Discussion Paper 3. Combating environmental degradation. Online:

http://www.unicc.org/ifad/envir.html International
Institute for Environment and Development (IIED)
(1992). Participatory rural appraisal for farmer
participatory research in Punjab, Pakistan. Report of a
training workshop. Pakistan-Swiss Potato Development
Project. Grjranwala, Punjab Province, Pakistan.
IRIS (1994). Draft project paper for project sustainability.
Institutional reform and the informal sector. MD:
University Park Isham, J., Narayan D., and Pritchett L.
(1995) Does participation improve performance?
Establishing causality with subjective data. The World
Bank Economic Review, 9 (2) 175-200.
Jacobs, M. (1991). The green economy. London: Pluto
Press.
Janzen, D. (1986). Guanacaste National Park: tropical
ecological and cultural restoration. San Jose, Costa Rica:
Editorial Universidad Estatal a Distancia. Johansson,
P.O., Kristrom, B. & Mäler, K.G. (Eds.) (1995). Current
issues in environmental economics. NY: Manchester
University Press.
Jordan, J.L. (1995). Incorporating externalities in
conservation programs. Journal of American Water
Works Association, 87 (6), 49-56.
Jurgen, K. (1995). The contribution of natural science
concepts to current discussion of order. Gestalt Theory,
17 (2), 153-163. Kanter, R.M. (1982). Dilemmas of
managing participation. Organizational Dynamics, 11 (1),
5-27.
Katz, D. & Kahn, R.L. (1966). Common characteristics of
open systems. In Systems thinking.
Emery F. (Ed.) (1981). Australia: Penguin Books Inc.
Victoria. Kerr, J. & Sanghi, N.K. (1992). Soil and water
conservation in India's semi-arid tropics. Sustainable
Agriculture Programme Gatekeeper Series SA34.
London:IIED. Kiel, L.D. (1994). Managing chaos and
complexity in government. CA: San Francisco Jossey-
Bass Inc. Publishers. Kimberly, J.R., & Bouchikhi, H.

(1995). The dynamics of organizational development and change: How the past shapes the present and constraints the future. Organization Science, 6 (1) 9-18. Kingdon, D.R. (1973). Matrix organization. Tavistock, London. Kohn, R.E. (1975). Air pollution control. Lexington Books. D.C. Lexington, Massachusetts: Heath and Company. Korten, D.C. (1980). Community organization and rural development: A learning process approach. Public Administration Review, 480-506. Kosslyn, S.M. & Osherson, D.N. (Eds) (1995). Visual Cognition. The MIT Press. Cambridge, Massachusetts.

Kottak, C.P. (1985). When people don't come first: Some sociological lessons from completed projects. In Putting People First. Sociological Variables in Rural Development. Michael Cernea, (Ed.). England: Oxford University Press.

Kranz H. (1976). The Participatory Bureaucracy. Lexington Books. D.C. Lexington, Massachusetts: Heath and Company. Kramer, J.T.A. (1977). Systems thinking. Leiden: Martinus Nijhoff Social Sciences Division. Langley, A., Mintzberg, H., Pitcher, P., Posada, E., & Saint-Macay, J. (1995). Opening up decision making: The view from the black stool. Organization Science, 6 (3) 260-279. Laroche, H. (1995). From decision to action in organizations: Decision-making as a social representation. Organization Science, 6 (1) 62-75. LATCO (1995). Economic News Ecuador.[Online]. Available e-mail: Latco@psg.com . Nov.1st, 1995. LBMF(1996). Long Beach Model Forest.[Online]. http://www.lbmf.bc.ca/index.html
Leff, E. (1994). Ecologia y capital: racionalidad ambiental, democracia participativa y desarrollo sustentable. Mexico: Siglo Veintiuno. _____ (1995). Green production. Toward an environmental rationality. New York: The Guildford Press. Lefroy, E.C., Salerian, J. & Hobbs, R.J. (1992) Integrating economic and ecological considerations: a theoretical framework. In

Reintegrating Fragmented Landscapes. Towards
Sustainable Production and Nature Conservation. R.J.
Hobbs and D.A. Saunders (Eds.). New York: Springer-
Verlag.

Levinson, H. (1970). Management by whose objectives?
Harvard Business Review. (July-August),pp.125-135.

Lewis, D., Kaweche, G.B.,& Mwenya, A. (1990).
Wildlife conservation outside protected areas-lessons
from an experiment in Zambia. Conserv. Biol., 4, 171-
80. Likert, R. (1958). Measuring organizational
performance. Harvard Business Review, March-April,
1958, 41-52. _____ (1967). The human organization.
New York:McGraw-Hill.

Lippitt, R. & White, R.K. (1943). The Social Climate of
Children's Groups. Child Behaviours & Development.
NY: McGraw-Hill. Litwin, M.S. (1995). How to measure
survey reliability and validity. CA: Sage Publications Inc.
Thousand Oaks.

Lloyd, A.L. (1995). Computing bouts of prisoner's
dilemma. Scientific American, 110-115.

Locke, E.A., Schweiger, D.M., & Latham, G.P. (1986).
Participation in decision- making: When should it be
used? Organizational Dynamics, 14 (3), 47-65.

Lowin, A. (1968). Participative decision making: A
model, literature critique, and prescriptions for research.
Organizational Behavior and Human Performance, 3, 68-
106. Lynch, O.J., & Talbott, K. (1995). Balancing Acts:
Community-based forest management and national law in
Asia and the Pacific. World Resources Institute.
Washington, D.C.

Macdonald, S. (1995). Learning to change: An
information perspective on learning in the organization.
Organization Science, 6 (5), 557-568.

Mainzer L.C. (1973). Political Bureaucracy. Glenview,
Illinois: Scott, Foresman and Company.

Malka, S. (1989). Managerial behavior, participation, and
effectiveness in social welfare organizations.

Administration in Social Work, 13 (2), 47-65.

Maskin, E.S. (1994). The invisible hand and externalities. American Economic Review, 84 (2), 333-337. Marchak, P. (1995). Logging the globe. McGill-Queen's University Press.

Marshall, A. 1947 (1890). Principles of Economics. London: Macmillan.

Maturana, H.R. & Varela, F.J. (1980). Autopoiesis & cognition. Dordrecht: Reidel.

McCaffrey D.P., Faerman, S.R., & Hart, D.W. (1995). The appeal and difficulties of participative systems. Organization Science, 6, (6), 603-627.

McMorran, R. T., & Nellor, D.C.L. (1994). Tax policy and the environment: theory and practice. IMF Working Paper. International Monetary Fund.

Meyer, M.W. (1977). Theory of organizational structure. Indianapolis: Bobbs-Merril Educational Publishing.

Mitchell & Carson (1995) Current issues in the design, administration, and analysis of contigent valuation surveys. In Johansson P., Kristrom B., and Maler K. (Eds.) Current issues in environmental economics. Manchester: Manchester University Press.

Montague, P. (1992) In the interests of others. An essay in moral philosophy. Philosophical Studies Series V.55. Boston: Kluwer Academic Publishers.

Morgan, G. (1986). Images of organizations. Newbury Park, CA:Sage Publications.

Mooney, J.D. (1939). The principles of organization. NY: Harper and Brothers.

Mott, P.E. (1972). The characteristics of effective organizations. NY: Harper and Row Publishers.

Myles, G.D. (1995). Public economics. Cambridge: University Press.

Narayan, D. (1995). The contribution of people's participation. Environmentally Sustainable Development Occasional Papers Series No.1. The World Bank: Washington, D.C..

Neuman, E. (1962). The origin and history of consciousness. Volume II. NY: Harper & Brothers.

Nohria, N. & Berkley, J.D. (1994). Whatever happened to the take-charge manager? Harvard Business Review, 72 (1), 128-137.

Nowak, M.A., May, R.M., & Sigmund, K. (1995). The arithmetics of mutual help. Scientific American, 76-81.

Norton, B.G. (1991). Ecological Health and sustainable resource management. In Ecological Economics: The science and management of sustainability, ed. Robert Costanza. New York: Columbia University Press.

O'Connor, J. (1997). Thinking past the obvious. On line: http://www.radix.net/~crbnblu/assoc/occonor/chapt1.htm

O'Riordan, T. (1976). Policy making and environmental management: Some thoughts on process and research issues. In Natural Resources for A Democratic Society: Public Participation in Decision-making. Utton, E.A., Derrick, W.R. & O'Riordan, T. (Eds). Boulder, Westview Press, 55-72.

Ormerod, P. (1995). The death of economics. NY:San Martin Press.

Osterfeld, D. (1994).The World Bank and the IMF. In The collapse of development planning. Boettke, P.J. (Ed.). New York: New York University Press.

Ostrom, E. (1990). Governing the commons: The evolution of institutions for collective action. UK: Cambridge. Cambridge University Press. Packard, T. (1989). Participation in decision-making, performance, and job satisfaction in a social work bureaucracy. Administration in Social Work, 13 (1), 59-73.

_____ (1993). Managers' and workers' views of the dimensions of participation in organizational decision-making. Administration in Social Work, 17 (2), 53- 65.

Papandreou, A.A. (1994). Externality and institutions. Oxford: Clareden Press.

Pepper, S. (1942). World hypotheses. CA: University of California Press. 1970.

Perrings, C. (1987). Economy and the environment: A theoretical essay on the interdependence of economic and environmental systems. Cambridge: Cambridge University Press.

Peters, C., & Nelson, M. (Eds.) (1979). The culture of bureaucracy. New York: Holt, Rinehart and Winston.

Peters, B.G., & Savoie, D.J. (Eds.) (1995) Governance in a changing environment. Canadian Centre for Management Development. McGill-Queen's University Press.

Pigou, A.C. (1962). The economics of welfare. Fourth Ed. London: Macmillan.

Pinchot, Gifford & Elizabeth (1993) The end of bureaucracy & the rise of the intelligent organization. San Francisco: Berrett-Keohler Publishers.

Pretty, J. N., Guijt, I., Shah, P., and Hindchcliffe, F. (1996). International Institute for Environment and Development. London, UK.

_____, Thompson, J., & Kiara, J.K. (1995) Agricultural regeneration in Kenya: the catchment approach to soil and water conservation. Ambio, 24 (1), 7.

_____.(1994). Alternative systems of inquiry for sustainable agriculture. Ids bulletin, 25 (2), 37-49.

Prychitko, D.L. (1993). Formalism in Austrian-school welfare economics: Another pretense of knowledge? Critical Review, 7 (4), 567-587.

Purser, R. (1997). Shallow versus deep organizational development and environmental sustainability. Journal of organizational change and development. On line: http://www.mcb.co.uk/services/articles/liblink/pubarti/joc m/purser.htm Ramón, G.V. (1993). Manual de planeamiento andino comunitario. El PAC en la region Andina. (2nd.ed.).Quito-Ecuador: COMUNIDEC.

_____, G.V. (1995). Las metodologias participativas en el Ecuador: entre la cooptación y el emploderamiento. Quito-Ecuador: COMUNIDEC.

Ramsdell, P.S. (1988). The relative benefits and costs to human service organization of staff participation in organizational decision-making. In National symposium on doctoral research and social work practice: Women's issues, poverty, and human service organizations. Columbus, OH: Ohio State University.

_____ (1994). Staff participation in organizational decision-making: An empirical study. Administration in Social Work, 18 (4), 51-69.

Ran, Y. (1985). Community forestry: Building success through people's participation. Unasylva. International Journal of Forestry and Forest Industries. FAO, 37 (147), 29-35.

Redclift, M. & Sage, C. (Eds.) (1994). Strategies for sustainable development. UK.: John Wiley & Sons.

Reinhard B. (1962). Max Weber: An intellectual portrait. Garden City, N.Y.: Doubleday Anchor Books.

Rehm, R.(1994). Participative design. Consortium for participative Democracy. Chicago: Loyola-Chicago University.

Repetto, R. (1990) Promoting environmentally sound economic progress: What the north can do. World Resources Institute.

Resnick, H., & Patti, R.J. (1980). Change from within: Humanizing social welfare organization. Philadelphia: Temple University Press.

Resnick, M. (1996). Beyond the Centralized Mindset. Journal of the Learning Sciences. 5 (1), 1-22.

_____ (1997) Learning about life. On line: http://el.www.media.mit.edu/groups/el/Papers/mres/ALife/ALife.html

Ruth, M. (1993) Integrating economics, ecology and thermodynamics. Boston: Massachusetts. Kluwer Academic Publishers.

Sachs, W. (1976). Toward formal foundations of teleological systems science. General Systems, 21.

Saltman, J.C. (1978). A primer on the construction and

testing of theories in sociology. Illinois: F.E. Peacock Publishing Inc.

Salwasser, H. (1994). Ecosystem management: can it sustain diversity and productivity? Journal of Forestry, 92, 6-11. Sashkin, M. (1986). Participative management remains an ethical imperative. Organizational Dynamics, 14 (4), 62-75. Sarri, R., and Sarri, C. (1992). Participatory action research in two communities in Bolivia and the United States. International Social Work, 35 (2), 267-80.

Schneider, H. (1988). Principles of development: A view from anthropology. In Production and Autonomy: Anthropological Studies and Critiques of Development, Monographs in Economic Anthropology, No.5. John Bennett and John Bowens (Eds.). University Press of America.

Senge, P. (1991). The fifth discipline: The art and practice of the learning organization. Cambridge, MA: Double Day. Shrivastava, P. (1983). A typology of organizational learning systems. Journal of Management Studies, 20 (1), 7-28. Shenhar, Y. (1995). From chaos to systems: The engineering foundations of organization theory, 1879-1932. Administrative Science Quarterly, 40, 557-585.

Siebert, H. (1981). Economics of the environment. D.C. Heath and Company. Lexington, Massachusetts.Toronto: Lexington Books.

Simon. H. (1991). Bounded rationality and organizational learning. Organization Science, 2 (1), 125-134.

Snyman, J.H. (1994). An empirical investigation of an integrative strategic management process model. Ph.D. diss. New Mexico State University. Las Cruces (Diss.Abstr. 94-123).

Sommerhoff, G. (1974). Logic of the living brain. London: John Wiley. Soros, G. (1996). The capitalist threat. The Atlantic monthly (Feb-97).

Southgate, D., & Whitaker, M. (1994). Economic Progress and the Environment. One Developing Country's

Policy Crisis. New York: Oxford University Press.

Spires, R.S. (1996) Personal communication. In Ecological Economics listserv

Stein, E.W. (1987). Participatory planning: An interactive management approach. AORN Journal, 46 (3), 508-517.

Templet, P.H. (1995). Grazing the commons: an empirical analysis of externalities, subsidies and sustainability. Ecological Economics, 12(2), 141-159.

Terry, L.D. (1995) Leadership of public bureaucracies. Sage Publications Inc. Thiertart, R.A., & Forgues, B. (1995). Chaos theory and organization. Organization Science, 1(1). Thompson, J. & Scones, I. (1994). Challenging the populist perspective: Rural people's knowledge, agricultural research, and extension practice. Agriculture and Human Values. 11 (2 & 3), 58-72.

Thrupp, L.A., Cabarle, B., & Zazueta, A. (1994). Participatory methods in planning and political processes: Linking the grassroots and policies for sustainable development. Agriculture and Human Values. 11 (2 & 3), 77-84.

Tisch, S.J., & Wallace, M.B. (1994). Dilemmas of development assistance. San Francisco: Westview Press, 1-116.

Toch, H., & Grant, J.D. (1982). Reforming human services: Change through participation. Beverly Hills: Sage Publications.

Trist, E., & Murray, H. (1993). The Social Engagement of Social Science: A Tavistock anthology. The sociotechnical perspective, V. 2. Philadelphia: University of Pennsylvania Press.

Trist, E.L. & Bamforth, K.W. (1951). Social and psychological consequences of the Longwall method of coal-getting. Human Relations, 4(1),3-38. Toman, M.A. (1994). Economics and "sustainability"; balancing trade-offs and imperatives. Land Economics, 70 (4), 399-413. Tulku, T. (1990). Knowledge of time and space. Berkeley, CA:

Dharma Publishing.

Turner, J.T. (1991). Participative management: Determining employee readiness. Administration and policy in Mental Health, 18 (5), 333-341. United Nations Development Commission (1993) Agenda 21: Action Plan for the Next Century. New York, (UNDC). UNEP (1995). Participatory development: A bottom-up approach to combating desertification. [Online] Fact Sheet 6. http://www.unep.ch/incd/fs6.html.

Upreti, G. (1994). Environmental conservation and sustainable development require a new development approach. Environmental Conservation, 21 (1), 18-29. Lausanne, Switzerland: Elsevier Science. USAID (1996). Strategic objectives for Ecuador. [Online]. Available e-mail

Gopher://gaia.info.usaid.gov:70/00/regional_country/lac/ecuador. USDA Forest Service (1995). Agroforestry and sustainable systems: Symposium proceedings. General Technical Report RM-GTR-261, July, 1995.

Usher, D. (1992). The welfare economics of markets, voting and predation. Ann Arbor: The University of Michigan Press. Utton, A.E., Sewel, W.R.D. & T. O'Riordan (Eds.) (1976). Natural Resources for a Democratic Society. Public Participation in Decision-Making. Boulder, Colorado: Westview Press.

Van Eijnatten, F.M. (1993). The Paradigm that changed the Work Place. Stockholm: The Swedish Center for Working Life. Van Pelt, M.J.F. (1993) Sustainability-Oriented Project Appraisal for Developing Countries. Rotterdam, Netherlands: Economics Research Foundation.

Vasquez, M.L. (1997). Avoidance strategies and governmental rigidity: the case of the small-scale shrimp fishery in two Mexican communities [Online] gopher://dizzy.library.arizona.edu:70/00/ej/PE/jpe/volume1/ascii/ascii-vasquez.txt

Von Amsberg, J. (1993). Project Evaluation and

Depletion of Natural Capital: An Application of the Sustainability Principle. The World Bank Environment Department. Working Paper No.56. WCED (1987). Our Common Future: The World Commission on Environment and Development. New York: Oxford University Press.

Weatherly, R.A. (1983). Participatory management in public welfare: What are the prospects? Administration in Social Work, 7 (1), 39-49. Weber, M. (1947). The theory of social and economic organization. NY: The Free Press. Weber, S., & Polm, D. (1974). Participatory management in public welfare. Social Casework, 55, 299-306.

Weick, K.E. (1991). The nontraditional quality of organizational learning. Organization Science, 2 (1), 116-124. Westley, F. & Vredenburg, H. (1996). Sustainability and the corporation. Journal of Management Inquiry. 5 (2), 104-119. Westoby, M., Walker, B., & Noy-Meir, I. (1989) Opportunistic management for rangelands not at equilibrium. Journal of Range Management. 42 (4), 266-274.

White, L.D. (1993). Trends in public administration. New York: McGregor-Hill

White, R. (1992). Towards a Green Political Economy: The Market. In Ronnie Harding, ed, Ecopolitics V Proceedings, CLGS, UNSW. Wichterman, Dana. (1995).Issue paper #2. Economic growth, Sustainability, and Sustainable Development. Document Paper: PN-ABU-374. Research and Reference Services Project. United States Agency for International Development. Center for Development Information and Evaluation. Washington D.C. 20523-1820. Wood, C.A. (1994-Spring). Ecosystem management: achieving the new land ethic. Renewable Resources Journal, 6-12. Wood, C.B. (1976). Conflict in resource management and the use of threat: The Goldstream controversy. In Natural Resources for A Democratic Society: Public Participation in Decision-making. Utton, E.A., Derrick, W.R. &

O'Riordan, T. (Eds). Boulder, Wetsview Press, 117-135 World Commission on Environment and Development (1987) Our Common Future. Oxford: Oxford university Press. World Bank (1995). Annual Review: Executive Summary. Report No.15085. [Online] http://WWW.WorldBank.org/html/oed/15084.html# World Resources Institute (WRI) (1993). Programa de Manejo Participativo de Recursos Naturales. Cuaderno Num.1. Instituto de los Recursos Mundiales, Washington D.C./Mexico, D.F.: Grupo de Estudios Ambientales A.C. Wynn, N. (1995). Alternative development strategies and regeneration of social space for human development. Peace & Change, 20. SAGE Publications Inc. Young, J.T. (1994). Entropy and natural resource scarcity: A reply to critics. Journal of Environmental Economics and Management, 26, 210-213.

Young, M.D. (1992). Sustainable Investment and Resource Use. Man and the Biosphere series. 9, 37-48.

APPENDIX A Survey Instrument
APPENDIX B Project Statistics
Project #1 Environmental Education Program Cost: ~$2,000 Location: Machalilla National Park (MNP) Financed by: USAID/The Nature Conservancy (TNC) Implemented by: Fundación Natura (FN) (Ecuadorian NGO) Date started: April 20, 1997 Date completed: October 20, 1997 Population Involved: 1 person Sample Interviewed: 1 person Project Objectives: To provide environmental education training for one individual.
Project #2 Solid Waste Disposal Cost: ~$5,000 Location: Agua Blanca, MNP Financed by: USAID/TNC Implemented by: FN Date started: July, 1996 Date completed: February, 1997 Population Involved: ~35 families Sample Interviewed: 21 individuals Objectives: To provide environmental education and a storage bunker for the proper collection, storage and recycling of solid waste in the community.
Project #3 Tagua Handcrafting Cost: ~$3,000 Location:

Agua Blanca Community, MNP Financed by:
TNC/USAID Implemented by: FN Date started: October,
1996 Date completed: December, 1996 Population
Involved: 5 individuals Population Interviewed: 3
individuals Objectives: To provide training, equipment,
and marketing for tagua handcrafting.
Project #4 Tourist Guide Training Cost: ~$10,000
Location: MNP Financed by: INEFAN, PNM
Implemented by: INEFAN/PNM Date started: June 9,
1997 Date completed: July 4, 1997 Population Involved:
33 people from different provinces and institutions
Sample interviewed: 3 individuals Objectives: To provide
education and training for naturalist tourist guides for the
PNM
Project #5 Tree Nursery Cost: ~$9,000 Location: Rio
Blanco, MNP Financed by: USAID/TNC Implemented
by: FN Date started: June, 1992 Date completed: July,
1996 Population Involved: ~30 families Sample
interviewed: 16 individuals Objectives: To provide
seedlings for reforestation.
Project #6 Galapagos Artisanal Fishing/SUBIR Cost:
~$650,000 Location: Galapagos Islands Financed by:
USAID PL-480 Implemented by: Charles Darwin
Research Station (CDRS) Date started: September, 1995
Date completed: December, 1997 Population Involved: ~
40 families Sample interviewed: 6 individuals Objectives:
1) Diffusion of Marine Reserve and, 2) Recycling
program.
Project #7 Galapagos Agroforestry/SUBIR Cost:
~$130,000 Location: Galapagos Islands (San Cristobal,
Santa Cruz, e Isabela) Financed by: USAID, 1990-1994;
PNUD, 1995; Canadian Fund, 1996-1997. Implemented
by: CDRS Date started: June, 1990 Date completed:
October, 1997 Population Involved: ~ 40 individuals
Sample Interviewed: 5 individuals Objectives: General:
Conservation and protection of Park. Specific: (1) Wiser
forestry use; (2) To replace areas occupied by invasive

species with safe species; (3) To plant a buffer zone to prevent the spread of other species.

Project #8.- Cayapas/Cotacachi Reserve/SUBIR Cost: ~$150,000 Location: Cayapas/Cotacachi Reserve (CCR) Financed by: USAID Implemented by: CARE International Date started: 1991 Date completed: 1997 Population Involved: ~100 families Sample interviewed: 35 individuals Objectives: To preserve the biodiversity of the reserve by developing and implementing a pilot plan for communal forest management that will provide economic alternatives while preserving natural resources.

Project#9 Desarrollo Forestal Campesino (DFC) Cost: ~$300,000 Location: Ecuadorian Andes Financed by: Food and Agriculture Organization (FAO) & The Netherlands Government Implemented by: INEFAN Date started: 1995 Date completed: on-going Population Involved: 150 families Sample interviewed: 9 individuals Objectives: to contribute to the improvement of the quality of life of Andean Peasants, especially women, helping them to get started in self-development and the sustainable use of their natural resources.

Made in the USA
Columbia, SC
25 February 2022